Biotechnology in the 21ˢᵗ Century

Biotechnology on the Farm and in the Factory
Agricultural and Industrial Applications

Biotechnology in the 21st Century

Biotechnology on the Farm and in the Factory
Agricultural and Industrial Applications

Biotechnology and Your Health
Pharmaceutical Applications

Bioinformatics, Genomics, and Proteomics
Getting the Big Picture

The Ethics of Biotechnology

Biotechnology in the 21ˢᵗ Century

Biotechnology on the Farm and in the Factory
Agricultural and Industrial Applications

Brian Shmaefsky

CHELSEA HOUSE
PUBLISHERS

CHELSEA HOUSE PUBLISHERS
VP, NEW PRODUCT DEVELOPMENT Sally Cheney
DIRECTOR OF PRODUCTION Kim Shinners
CREATIVE MANAGER Takeshi Takahashi
MANUFACTURING MANAGER Diann Grasse

Staff for BIOTECHNOLOGY ON THE FARM AND IN THE FACTORY
EDITOR Beth Reger
PRODUCTION EDITOR Bonnie Cohen
PHOTO EDITOR Sarah Bloom
SERIES & COVER DESIGNER Keith Trego
LAYOUT 21st Century Publishing and Communications, Inc.

www.chelseahouse.com

First Printing

9 8 7 6 5 4 3 2 1

Library of Congress Cataloging-in-Publication Data

Shmaefsky, Brian.
   Biotechnology in the farm and factory: agricultural and industrial applications/Brian Shmaefsky.
      p. cm.—(Biotechnology in the 21st century)
   Includes bibliographical references.
   ISBN 0-7910-8518-X (alk. paper)
1. Agricultural biotechnology. 2. Biotechnology. I. Title. II. Series.
S494.5.B563S53 2005
664'.024—dc22

                                                                        2005011990

Table of Contents

Detailed Table of Contents

Foreword

The processes that eventually led to life began inside the first generation of stars that resulted after what astrophysicists refer to as the Big Bang. The events associated with the Big Bang mark the beginning of our universe—a time during which such simple elements as hydrogen and helium were turned by gravitational pressure and heat into carbon, oxygen, nitrogen, magnesium, chlorine, calcium, sodium, sulfur, phosphorous, iron, and other elements that would make the formation of the second generation of stars and their planets possible. The most familiar of these planets, our own planet Earth, would give rise to life as we know it—from cells and giant squids to our own human race.

At every step in the processes that led to the rich variety of life on Earth, the thing that was forming in any particular environment was capable of transforming, and did, transform that environment. Especially effective at transformation was that class of things that we now refer to as replicators. We know of two examples of replicators: genes and memes. (The latter rhymes with "creams.")

Genes and memes exist in cells, tissues, and organs. But memes mostly are in brains, and human religions and civilizations. Near the bottom of the hierarchy it's all genes and near the top it's more memes. Genes appeared independently of cells, and are responsible for most of what we call biological life, which can be thought of as a soft and comfortable vehicle made mostly of cells, and created and maintained by the genes, for their efficient replication and evolution. Amazingly, the existence of replicators is all it takes to explain life on Earth; no grand creation, no intelligent design, no constant maintenance; at first just genetic replicators and natural selection, and as far as we know, just one more thing, which appeared after there were human brains big enough to support them: memes.

Genes you've already heard of; but memes may be a completely new term to you. Memes follow the same rules as genes and their natural selection and evolution account for everything that the natural selection of genes doesn't. For instance, our brains are almost too large for our upright stance and therefore must somehow answer to a calling other than the mere replication of our genes, which were doing okay without the extra pint of white matter we gained in the last 50,000 years. The striking increase in brain size means something powerful is strongly benefiting from our increased brain capacity. The best explanation for this, according to Richard Dawkins, in his best-selling and robustly influential book, *The Selfish Gene*, is that our brains are particularly well adapted for imitation, and therefore for the replication of memes. Memes are things like words, ideas, songs, religious or political viewpoints, and nursery rhymes. Like genes, they exist for themselves—that is, they are not here to promote us or anything else, and their continued existence does not necessarily depend on their usefulness to anything: only to their fecundity, their ability to copy themselves in a very precise, but inexact way, and their relative stability over time. It is these features of **genes** and of **memes** that allow them to take part in natural selection, as described by Darwin in 1859, in spite of the fact that he was unaware of the nature of the two replicators. After 150 years, we have started to understand the details. Looking back on it from only a century and a half, Darwin's conception was probably the most brilliant that mankind has chanced upon in our relatively short time here on Earth. What else could possibly explain dandelions?

Dawkins realized that the genes were evolving here, not us. We are just the vessel, and Dawkins realized the significance of replicators in general. After that, the field opened up rather widely, and must include Stan Cohen and Herbert Boyer, whose notion, compounded in 1973 in a late-night deli in Oahu, of artificially replicating specific genes underlies most of the subject matter in this rather important series of books.

SO WHAT'S SO IMPORTANT ABOUT GENES AND MEMES?

I'm sure that most of you might want to know a little bit about the stuff from which you are made. Reading the books in this series will teach you about the exciting field of biotechnology and, perhaps, most importantly, will help you understand what you are (now pay attention, the following clause sounds trivial but it isn't), *and* give you something very catchy to talk about with others, who will likely pass along the information to others, and so on. What you say to them may outlive you. Reading the books in this series will expose you to some highly contagious memes (recall that memes are words, ideas, etc.) about genes. And you will likely spread these memes, sometimes without even being aware that you are doing so.

THE BIRTH OF BIOTECHNOLOGY—OAHU 1973

So what happened in Oahu in 1973? Taking the long view, nothing really happened. But we rarely take the long view, so let's take the view from the 70s.

At the time, it was widely held that genes belonged to a particular organism from whose progenitors the gene had been passed to an organism and that the organism in question would pass the gene to its offspring, and that's the only way that genes got around. It made sense. Genes were known by then to carry the instructions for building new organisms out of the germinal parts of old organisms, including constructing a wide array of devices for collecting the necessary raw materials needed for the process from the environment; genes were the hereditary mechanism whereby like begat like, and you looked like your parents because of similar genes, rather than looking like your neighbors. The "horizontal transfer" of genes from one species to another was not widely contemplated as being possible or desirable, in spite of the fact that such transfer was already evident in the animal and plant worlds—think of mules and nectarines. And "undesirable" is putting it rather mildly. A lot of people thought it was a horrible idea. I was a research scientist in the recombinant laboratories of Cetus Corporation in 1980, during which time Cetus management prudently did not advertise the location of the lab for fear that the good people of Berkeley, California (a town known for its extreme tolerance of most things) might take offense and torch our little converted warehouse of a lab. Why this problem in regard to hybrid life forms? Maybe it had something to do with the fact that mules were sterile and nectarines were fruit.

Apples have been cultivated in China for at least 4,000 years. The genetic divergence from the parental strains has all been accomplished by intentional cultivation, including selection of certain individuals for properties that appealed to our farming ancestors; and farmers did so without much fanfare. The Chinese farmers were not aware that genes were being altered permanently and that was the reason that the scions from favored apple trees, when grafted onto a good set of roots, bred true. But they understood the result. Better apple genes have thus been

continually selected by this process, although the process throughout most of history was not monitored at the genetic level. The
farmers didn't have any scary words to describe what they were
doing, and so nobody complained. Mules and nectarines and
Granny Smith apples were tolerated without anyone giving a hoot.

Not so when some educated biologists took a stab at the same
thing and felt the need to talk about it in unfamiliar terms to each
other, but not the least to the press and the businessmen who were
thinking about buying in. There was, perhaps, a bit too much
hyperbole in the air. Whatever it was, nobody was afraid of apples,
but when scientists announced that they could move a human gene
into a bacterium, and the bacterium would go on living and copying
the gene, all hell broke loose in the world of biology and the sleepy
little discipline of bioethics became a respectable profession. Out of
the settling dust came the biotechnology industry, with recombinant
insulin, human growth hormone, erythropoietin, and tissue plas-
minogen activator, to name a few.

CETUS IN 1980

The genie was out of the bottle. Genes from humans had been put
into terrified bacteria and the latter had survived. No remarkable
new bacteremias—that is, diseases characterized by unwanted
bacteria growing in your blood—had emerged, and the initial
hesitancy to do recombinant DNA work calmed down. Cetus built
a P-3, which was something like an indoor submarine, with labs
inside of it. The P-3 was a royal pain to get in and out of; but it had
windows through which potential investors could breeze by and
be impressed by the bio-suited scientists and so, just for the
investment it encouraged, it was worth it. Famous people like Paul
Berg at Stanford had warned the biotech community that we were
playing with fire. It stimulated investment. When nobody died
bleeding from the eyeballs, we started thinking maybe it wasn't
all that scary. But there was something in the air. Even the janitors

pushing their brooms through the labs at night and occasional scientists working until dawn, felt that something new and promising was stirring.

My lab made oligonucleotides, which are little, short, single-stranded pieces of DNA, constructed from the monomers A, C, T, and G that we bought in kilogram quantities from the Japanese, who made them from harvested salmon sperm (don't ask me how). We broke these DNA pieces down into little nucleoside constituents, which we chemically rebuilt into 15- to 30-base long sequences that the biologists at Cetus could use to find the big pieces, the genes, that coded for things like interferons, interleukins, and human proteins.

We were also talking about turning sawdust into petroleum products. The price of petroleum in the world was over $35 a barrel, if my memory serves me at all, which was high for the decade. A prominent oil company became intrigued with the sawdust to petroleum idea and gave us somewhere between $30 or $40 million to get us started on our long-shot idea.

The oil company funding enabled us to buy some very expensive, sensitive instruments, like a mass spectrometer mounted on the backside of a gas chromatograph, now called GCMS. It was possible under very special conditions, using GCMS, to prove that it could be done—glucose could be converted biologically into long chain hydrocarbons. And that's what gasoline was, and sawdust was mainly cellulose, which was a polymer of glucose, so there you have it. Wood chips into gasoline by next year. There were a few details that have never been worked out, and now it has been a quarter of a very interesting century in which the incentive, the price of oil, is still very painful.

My older brother Brent had gone to Georgia Tech as had I. He finished in chemical engineering and I in chemistry. Brent worked for a chemical company that took nitrogen out of the air and methane out of a pipe and converted them into just about anything from fertilizer to the monomers needed to make things like nylon and polyethylene. Brent and I both knew about chemical plants, with their miles of pipes and reactors and about a century of good technical improvements, and that the quantities of petroleum products necessary to slake the global appetite for dark, greasy things would not fit easily into indoor submarines. We had our doubts about the cellulose to oil program, but proteins were a different thing altogether. Convincing bacteria, then later yeasts and insect cells in culture, to make human proteins by inserting the proper genes not only seemed reasonable to us but it was reasonable.

WE DID IT!

I remember the Saturday morning when David Mark first found an *E. coli* clone that was expressing the DNA for human beta-interferon using a P32 labeled 15-base long oligonucleotide probe that my lab had made. Sometimes science is really fun. I also remember the Friday night driving up to my cabin in Mendocino County when I suddenly realized you could make an unlimited amount of any DNA sequence you had, even if what you had was just a tiny part of a complex mixture of many DNAs, by using two oligos and a polymerase. I called it Polymerase Chain Reaction. The name stuck, but was shortened to PCR.

We were down in a really bad part of town, Emeryville being the industrial side of Berkeley; but we were young and brave, and sometimes it was like an extended camping trip. There were train tracks behind our converted warehouse. You could walk down them during the daytime to an Indian restaurant for lunch, or if you could manage to not be run over by a train late at night while a gel was running or an X-ray plate was exposing, you could creep over across the tracks to the adjacent steel mill and watch white hot steel pouring out of great caldrons. In the evenings, you could go up on the roof and have a beer with the president of the company.

Like the Berkeley of the late Sixties which had preceded it, it was a time that would never happen again.

Today, nobody would be particularly concerned about the repercussions of transferring a gene out of bacteria, say a gene out of *Bacillus thuringiensis* inserted into a commercial strain of corn, for instance. Genes now have found a new way to be moved around, and although the concept is not revolutionary, the rate at which it is happening is much faster than our own genes can react to. The driver, which is the case for all social behaviors in humans today, is the meme. Memes can appear, replicate, and direct our actions as fast as thought. It isn't surprising, but it does come as a shock to many people when they are confronted with the undisputed fact that the evolving elements in what we have referred to as biological evolution, which moves us from *Homo habilus* to *Homo sapiens*, are genes; not organisms, packs, species, or kinship groups. The things that evolve are genes, selfishly. What comes as an even more shocking surprise, and which in fact is even less a part of the awareness of most of us, is that our behavior is directed by a new replicator in the world, the meme.

YOU MAY WANT TO SKIP THIS PART
(Unless You're Up for Some Challenging Reading)

Let's digress a little, because this is a lot of new stuff for some people and may take a few hours to soak in. For starters, what exactly is a gene? . . . atgaagtgtgccgtgaaagctgctacgctcgacgctc-gatcacctggaaaaccctggtag . . . could be the symbol for a gene, a rather short gene for our editorial convenience here (most of them have thousands of letters). This rather short gene would code for the peptide met-lys-cys-ala-val-lys-gly-gly-thr-leu-asp-ala-arg-ser-pro-gly-lys-pro-trp, meaning that in a cell, it would direct the synthesis of that string of amino acids, (which may or may not do something very important).

Getting back to the gene, it may share the organism as an environment favoring its replication with a whole gang of other replicators (genes), and they may cooperate in providing a comfy little protected enclave in which all of the genes develop a means to replicate and cast their sequences into the future all using the same mechanism. That last fact is important as it separates a cellular gene from a viral gene, but I won't belabor it here. Reviewing just a little of what I've infected you with, that sequence of AGCT-type letters above would be a replicator, a gene, if it did the following:

(1) exhibited a certain level of fecundity—in other words, it could replicate itself faster than something almost like it that couldn't keep up;

(2) its replication was almost error-free, meaning that one generation of it would be the same as the next generation with perhaps a minor random change that would be passed on to what now would be a branch of its gene family, just often enough to provide some variation on which natural selection could act; and

(3) it would have to be stable enough relative to the generation time of the organism in which it found itself, to leave, usually unchanged, with its companion genes when the organism reproduced.

If the gene goes through the sieve of natural selection successfully, it has to have some specific identity that will be preserved long enough so that any advantage it confers to the rate of its own replication will, at least for some number of generations, be associated with its special identity. In the case of an organic replicator, this specialness will normally be conferred by the linear sequence of letters, which describe according to the genetic code, a linear sequence of amino acids in a peptide. The process is self-catalytic and almost irreversible, so once a sequence exhibits some advantage in either (1), (2), or (3), all other things being nearly equal, it is selected. Its less fortunate brethren are relatively unselected and the new kid on the block takes over the whole neighborhood. See how that works?

This should not be shocking to you, because it is a tautology, meaning it implies nothing new. Some people, however, are accustomed to the notion that genes and individual organisms serve the greater good of something they call a species, because in the species resides an inviolate, private gene pool, which is forever a part of that species. This concept, whether you like it or not, is about as meaningful—and now I guess I will date myself—as the notion that Roger Waters is forever and always going to be playing with Pink Floyd. It isn't so. Waters can play by himself or more likely with another group. So can genes. And don't forget that not only genes, but also an entirely different kind of replicator is currently using our bodies as a base of operations. Genes have a reaction time that is slow relative to the lifetime of an individual. It takes a long time for genes to respond to a new environment. Memes can undergo variation and selection at the speed of thought.

Let's leave the subject of memes for awhile. They are an immense part of every human now, but biotechnology as practiced in the world and described in this book does not pay them much mind. Biotechnologists are of the impression that their world is of genes, and that's alright. A whole lot happened on Earth before anybody even expected that the place was spinning and moving through space, so memes can wait. I thought I ought to warn you.

It is worth noting that new gene *sequences* arise from preexisting gene sequences but gene *molecules* are not made out of old genes. Gene molecules are made out of small parts that may have been in genes before, but the atoms making up the nucleotides that are strung together and constitute today's incarnation of a gene, may have two weeks ago been floating around in a swamp as urea or flying out of a volcano as hot lava. A gene *sequence* (notice that molecule is not equal to sequence) that makes itself very useful may last millions of years with hardly a single change. You may find precisely the same gene sequence in a lot of very different species with few significant changes because that sequence codes for some protein like cytochrome C that holds an iron atom in a particularly useful way, and everybody finds that they need it. It's a more classic design than a Jaguar XK and it just keeps on being useful through all kinds of climatic eras and in lots of different species. The sequence is almost eternal. On the very different other hand, the specific molecular incarnations of a gene sequence, like the DNA molecule that encodes the cytochrome C sequence in an individual cell of the yeast strain that is used, for example, to make my favorite bread, Oroweat Health Nut, is ephemeral. The actual molecules strung together so accurately by the DNA polymerase to make the cytochrome C are quickly unstrung in my small intestine as soon as I have my morning toast. I just need the carbon, nitrogen, and phosphorous. I don't eat it for the sequence. All DNA sequences taste the same, a little salty if you separate them from the bread.

That's what happens to most chemical DNA molecules. Somebody eats them and they are broken down into general purpose biological building blocks, and find their way into a new and different molecule. Or, as is often the case in a big organism like Arnold Schwarzenegger, body cells kill themselves while Governor Schwarzenegger is still intact because of constantly undergoing perfectly normal tissue restructuring. Old apartments come down, new condos go up, and beautiful, long, perfectly replicated DNA sequences are taken apart brick by brick. It's dangerous stuff to leave around on a construction site. New ones can be made. The energy just keeps coming: the sun, the hamburgers, the energy bars.

But the master sequences of replicators are not destroyed. Few germ cells in a woman's ova and an embarrassingly large number of germ cells in a male's sperm are very carefully left more or less unaltered, and I say more or less, because one of the most important processes affecting our genes, called recombination, does alter the sequences in important ways; but I'm not going to talk about it here, because it's pretty complicated and this is getting to be too long. Now we are ready to go back to the big question. It's a simple answer, but I don't think you are going to get it this year.

If . . . atgaagtgtgccgtgaaagctgctacgctcgacgctcgatcacctggaaaaccct-ggtag . . . is a gene, then what particular format of it is a gene? For this purpose, let's call it a replicator instead of a gene, because all genes are after all replicators. They happen to encode protein sequences under certain conditions, which is one of our main uses for them. As I've mentioned, the one above would code for the protein met-lys-cys-ala-val-lys-gly-gly-thr-leu-asp-ala-arg-ser-pro-gly-lys-pro-trp with the final "tag" being a punctuation mark for the synthesis mechanism to stop. We make other uses of them. There are DNA aptamers, which are single-stranded DNA polymers useful for their three-dimensional structures and ability to specifically cling to particular molecular structures, and then there is CSI, where DNA is used purely for its ability to distinguish between individuals. But *replication* for the genes is their reason for being here. By "reason for being here," I don't mean to imply that they are here because they had some role to fulfill in some overall scheme; I just mean simply that they are here because they replicate—it's as simple or impossible to understand as that. Their normal way of replication is by being in their molecular form as a double stranded helical organic polymer of adenosine, guanosine, thymidine, and cytosine connected with phosphate linkages in a cell. Or they could be in a PCR tube with the right mixture of nucleoside triphosphates, simple inorganic salts, DNA polymerase, and short strands of single-stranded DNA called primers (we're getting technical here, that's why you have to read these books). Looking ahead, DNA polymerase is a molecular machine that hooks the triphosphate form of four molecular pop beads called A, C, T, and G together into long meaningful strings.

Okay, getting back to the question, is the gene, . . . atgaagtgtgccgtgaaagctgctacgctcgacgctcgatcacctggaaaaccctggtag . . . always the organic polymer form of the sequence, which has a definite mass, molecular weight, chemical structure, or is the Arabic letter form of it in your book still a gene, or is the hexadecimal representation of it, or the binary representation of it in your CPU a gene, or is an equivalent series of magnetic domains aligned in a certain way on your hard disk just another form of a gene? It may sound like a dumb question, but it isn't. If you are insistent that a gene is just the organic polymer of A, C, T, and G that can be operated on by DNA polymerase to make replicas in a cell, then you may take a minute to think about the fact that those little triphosphate derivatives of A, C, T, and G may not have been little nucleotides last month when they were instead disembodied nucleotide pieces or even simple atoms. The atoms may have been residing in things called sugars or amino acids in some hapless organism that happened to become food for a bigger organism that contained the machinery that assembled the atoms into nucleotides, and strung them into the sequence of the gene we are talking about. The thing that is the same from generation to generation is the sequence, not the molecule. Does that speak to you? Does it say something like maybe the symbol of the gene is more the gene than the polymer that right now contains it, and the comprehensive symbolic representation of it in any form at all is a replicator? This starts to sound pretty academic, but in any biotechnology lab (and you will read about some of them in this series) making human proteins to sell for drugs, the genes for the proteins take all the above mentioned forms at one time or another depending on what is appropriate, and each of them can be reasonably called a replicator, the gene. Genetic engineering is not just the manipulation of chemicals.

SKIP DOWN TO HERE

These books are not written to be the behind the scenes story of genes and memes any more than a description of an integrated circuit for someone who wants to use it in a device for detecting skin conductivity or radio waves is about quantum mechanics. Quantum mechanics is how we understand what's happening inside of a transistor embedded in an integrated circuit in your iPod or described in the Intel catalogue. By mentioning what's going on inside biotechnology, I hope to spark some interest in you about what's happening on the outside, where biotechnology is, so you can get on about the important business of spreading these memes to your friends. There's nothing really thrilling about growing bacteria that make human hormones, unless your cousin needs a daily injection of recombinant insulin to stay alive, but the whole process that you become involved in when you start manipulating living things for money or life is like nothing I've found on the planet for giving you the willies. And remember what I said earlier: you need something to talk about if you are to fulfill your role as a meme machine, and things that give you the willies make great and easily infectious memes. Lowering myself to the vernacular for the sake of the occasional student who has made it this far, "biotech is far out man." If you find something more interesting, let me know. I'm at kary@karymullis.com, usually.

Dr. Kary B. Mullis
Nobel Prize Winner in Chemistry, 1993
President/Altermune, LLC

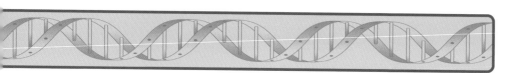

Introduction

Biotechnology, the use of biological organisms and processes to provide useful products in industry and medicine, is as old as cheese making and as modern as creating a plant-based energy cell or the newest treatment for diabetes. Everyday, newspaper articles proclaim a new application for biotechnology. Often, the media raises alarms about the potential for new kinds of biotechnology to harm the environment or challenges our ethical values. As a result of conflicting information, sorting through the headlines can be a daunting task. These books are designed to allow you to do just that—by providing the right tools to help you to make better educated judgments.

The new biotechnologies share with the old a focus on helping people lead better, safer, and healthier lives. Older biotechnologies, such as making wine, brewing beer, and even making bread, were based on generations of people perfecting accidental discoveries.

The new biotechnologies are built on the explosion of discoveries made over the last 75 years about how living things work. In particular, how cells use genetic material to direct the production of proteins that compose them, and provide the engines used to produce energy needed to keep them alive. These discoveries have allowed scientists to become genetic engineers, enabling them to move genes from one living organism to another and change the proteins made by the new organism, whether it is a bacterium, plant, mouse, or even a human.

Biotechnologists first engineered bacterial cells, producing new proteins useful in medicine and industry. The type of cell that biotechnologists engineer today may be a simple bacterium or a complicated animal or human cell. The protein product might be a simple string of amino acids or a complicated antibody of four chains, with critical genetic instructions from both mice and humans. Plant biotechnologists engineer plants to resist predatory insects or harmful chemicals to help farmers produce more, with less risk and expense. Plants have also been engineered to make products useful for industry and manufacturing. Animals have been engineered for both research and practical uses.

Research is also underway to develop methods of treating human diseases by changing the genetic information in the cells and tissues in a patient's body. Some of these efforts have been more successful than others and some raise profound ethical concerns. Changing the genetic information of a human may one day prevent the development of disease, but the effort to do so pushes the envelope of both ethics and technology. These and other issues raised by advances in biotechnology demand that we as citizens understand this technology, its promise, and its challenge so that we can provide appropriate limits on what biotechnologists create.

Who are the biotechnologists, the genetic engineers? Generally, they have university or advanced training in biology or chemistry. They may work in a university, a research institute, a company, or the government. Some are laboratory scientists trained in the tools of genetic engineering–the laboratory methods that allow a gene for a particular protein to be isolated from one living creature's DNA and inserted into another's DNA in a way that instructs the new cell to manufacture the protein. Some are computer scientists who assemble databases of the DNA and protein sequences of whole organisms. They may write the computer code that allows other scientists to explore the databases and use the information to gain understanding of evolutionary relationships or make new discoveries. Others work in companies that engineer biological factories to produce medicines or industrial plastics. They may engineer plants to promote faster growth and offer better nutrition. A few have legal training that allows them to draft or review patents that are critical to the business of biotechnology. Some even work in forensic laboratories, processing the DNA fingerprinting you see on TV.

The exact number of working biotechnologists is hard to determine, since the job description doesn't neatly fit into a conventional slot. The U.S. Department of Labor indicates that there are over 75,000 Master's and Ph.D.-level biologists in the U.S. and Bio.org, the Website for the Biotechnology Industry Organization, reports nearly 200,000 biotechnologists are currently employed.

Biotechnology is not just the stuff of the future. The work of modern biotechnology and genetic engineering is in our daily lives, from the food we eat and clothing we wear to some of the medicines we take. The ketchup you put on your fries at lunch today may have been sweetened with corn syrup made from corn that was engineered to resist a deadly insect. The cotton in your T-shirt, even if the shirt were made in China or Bangladesh, probably came from a U.S. cotton plant genetically engineered to resist another insect. If someone in your family is a diabetic, the insulin he or she injects and the glucose test monitor used to determine the amount of insulin to inject rely on biotechnology. If you go to the doctor and she arranges for blood tests, the laboratory uses biotechnology products to run those tests.

This series, BIOTECHNOLOGY IN THE 21ST CENTURY, was developed to allow you to understand the tools and methods of biotechnology, and to appreciate the current impact and future applications of biotechnology in agriculture, industry, and your health. This series also provides an exploration of how computers are used to manage the enormous amount of information produced by genetic researchers. The ethical and moral questions raised by the technology, whether they involve changing the genetic information of living things or using cells from human embryos to develop new ways to treat disease, are posed with a foundation in how moral philosophers think about ethical issues. With these tools, you will be better able to understand the headlines about the latest advances in biotechnology and the alarms raised by those concerned with the impact that these applications have on the environment and our society. You may even be inspired to learn more and join the community of scientists who work on finding new and better ways to produce food, products, and medical treatments.

Bernice Zeldin Schacter, Ph.D.
Consulting Editor

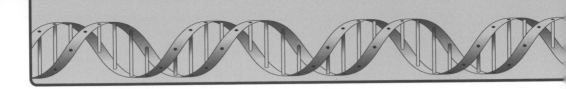

1

The Role of Biotechnology in Everyday Life

WHAT IS MODERN AGRICULTURE?

What would our lives be like without modern agriculture? Imagine going to the grocery store and finding that the produce section lacked your favorite fruits and vegetables. Then think about buying an apple and finding out that it costs over two dollars. Now, imagine that the apple is small, soft, and has lots of broken skin. Finally, picture yourself biting into the apple only to find that you have just taken in a mouthful of juicy caterpillar. This may not sound like an appealing story, but it is one that would be all too common if modern agriculture did not exist. Agriculture began in the Mediterranean area at least 10,000 years ago. It involved nothing more than growing fields of local plants and keeping pens of wild animals (Figure 1.1). Agriculture today is not that easy.

People developed agriculture when older methods of gathering food were not adequate to feed the growing populations settling in

Figure 1.1 Ancient agriculture involved the care of wild animals and plants raised in fields near the cities or villages. It was typical to have a variety of wild animals roaming around in fenced off areas. Some animals were bred for domestication as shown in this Egyptian wall painting. Different animals and crops were domesticated at first in the "Old Word" and in the "New World."

cities. Initially, people used hunting and gathering methods to feed small populations. That is, people hunted animals and gathered local plants to use for food. This strategy, however, was not an effective means for feeding large populations living in a small area. The continuous collecting of animals and plants caused food shortages. It became necessary to travel farther and farther to gather food. This became a big problem when people from different regions started competing for the same food. Eventually, people discovered that they could get abundant supplies of food more easily by growing or raising it themselves on farms.

Modern agriculture got its start long before people were aware of the science behind their ideas. By observing the types of offspring produced by captive animals, people were able to cultivate the animals and crops they needed to survive. As cities grew, however, fewer people practiced agriculture. Many took on other trades. To meet the needs of the whole population, people had to produce food more effectively. Thus, they found ways to produce more food in less space. They bred plants and animals that grew faster, bigger, and better. They developed ways to enhance the growth of plants and animals. They found ways to protect the plants and animals from damage and injury by pests. Even with these advancements, however, keeping people fed became more difficult as civilizations grew and started to live in large, sprawling cities.

The use of new technologies to increase productivity gave rise to modern agriculture. Tractors and harvesters modeled after trucks and military vehicles helped farmers grow more crops. New findings in chemistry led to the development of pesticides (chemicals that kill pests) for preventing damage and disease to crops and animals. Chemistry also provided a better understanding of plant growth, leading to the introduction of fertilizers for crops. Similar findings gave rise to special feeds for animals. Developments such as refrigeration made it possible to store food and to ship it long distances without risk of spoilage.

By the 1950s, modern agriculture reached a point where there were no new technologies available to further increase animal and crop production. Yet, it became more import to produce more food per farm as industrial facilities, recreational areas, and suburbs replaced agricultural lands. Farms needed to be more productive. Additionally, there was growing criticism that modern agricultural practices were polluting the Earth. Society needed to find creative technologies for increasing food production without hurting the Earth. It was biotechnology that provided this technology.

WHAT IS AGRICULTURAL BIOTECHNOLOGY?

The term **biotechnology** must first be defined before we can under-stand how it is applied to agriculture. Biotechnology is the utilization of the chemistry of living **organisms** in much the same way that technology and machinery are used in high-tech applications. In its simplest form, *agricultural biotechnology* means replacing manu-factured pesticides with chemicals derived from plants or animals. People have used this form of biotechnology for thousands of years, to different extents. Many foods and beverages were, and still are, made with the help of organisms, such as bread, summer sausage, yogurt, and wine which utilize **yeasts** or **bacteria.**

Genetic engineering is a more complicated form of biotechnology. Through this process, an organism is changed at its most basic **biochemical** level in a way that gives the organism a desirable trait (such as the bright red color of ripe tomoatoes) or removes an undesirable trait (rapid decomposition of tomoatoes, for example). An organism changed in this way (genetically) is called a **genetically modified organism**, or **GMO**. Genetic engineering can give a plant the ability to resist pests without pesticides or to produce more nutrients without the need for artificial fertilizers. GMOs can even reduce the need for farm machinery in some cases. Certain plants are being created which do not require as much fertilizer and pest control agents as current crops. This would reduce the number of times that a tractor must be driven across a field to spread the agricultural chemicals, saving on fuel and maintence costs. It is also possible to produce plants the need less water, reducing the need to irrigate.

What part of an organism's chemisty is used in agricultural biotechnology? Organisms are made up of four types of bio-chemical **molecules: carbohydrates, fats, proteins,** and **nucleic acids**

(Figure 1.2). Carbohydrates are commonly called "sugars." Simple carbohydrates called "monosaccharides" (one sugar) act as fuel for most organisms. They are used to run an organism's **metabolism.** Carbohydrates called "polysaccharides" (many monosaccharies linked together) make up a large variety of chemicals. Starch is one of the more common polysaccharides. Only plants produce starch. The fibers found in many types of fabrics and in wood are also polysaccharides. Other carbohydrates act as natural glues and preservatives. Ice cream and many desserts contain these carbohydrates. They help delay spoiling and prevent foods from melting too quickly. Scientists are currently using agricultural biotechnology to grow plants that produce unique types of fibers made from polysaccharides. These fibers can be used to make durable building materials and **biodegradable** fabrics.

Fats are simple chemicals made up of carbon, hydrogen, and oxygen atoms. All organisms need fats to help hold together their cells. Fats are also stored in the cells of organisms as food reserves, which are critical for keeping the body going when energy demands exceed the available nutrients. Many **hormones** (chemicals that control how cells do their jobs) are also categorized as fats. Many plants contain different types of fats known as oils. These oils have a variety of uses in everyday life. Plant oils can be found in many household materials, including paints and plastics. Some oils are used to lubricate machines and are even capable of being used as fuel in place of petroleum. Scientists are currently exploring the use of agricultural biotechnology to grow plants capable of producing petroleum products such as gasoline to run cars and other machines.

Proteins are complex chemicals made up of chains of **amino acids.** Plants produce amino acids when they take up fertilizer. Animals get their proteins by eating the amino acids in the proteins of plants and other animals. Proteins help build the cells and **tissues** of organisms. Fingernails and toenails are composed of

(continued on page 8)

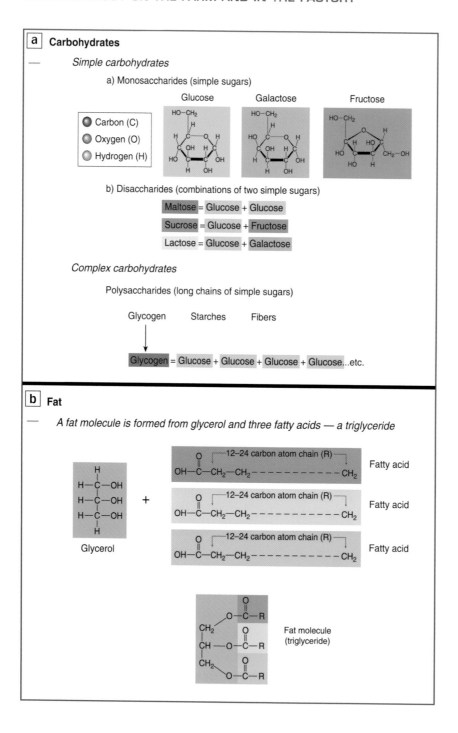

a | **Carbohydrates**

— *Simple carbohydrates*

a) Monosaccharides (simple sugars)

Glucose   Galactose   Fructose

● Carbon (C)
● Oxygen (O)
● Hydrogen (H)

b) Disaccharides (combinations of two simple sugars)

Maltose = Glucose + Glucose

Sucrose = Glucose + Fructose

Lactose = Glucose + Galactose

Complex carbohydrates

Polysaccharides (long chains of simple sugars)

Glycogen   Starches   Fibers

Glycogen = Glucose + Glucose + Glucose + Glucose...etc.

b | **Fat**

— *A fat molecule is formed from glycerol and three fatty acids — a triglyceride*

12–24 carbon atom chain (R)

$OH-C-CH_2-CH_2- - - - - - - - - - - CH_2$ Fatty acid

12–24 carbon atom chain (R)

$OH-C-CH_2-CH_2- - - - - - - - - - CH_2$ Fatty acid

12–24 carbon atom chain (R)

$OH-C-CH_2-CH_2- - - - - - - - - - CH_2$ Fatty acid

Glycerol   +

Fat molecule
(triglyceride)

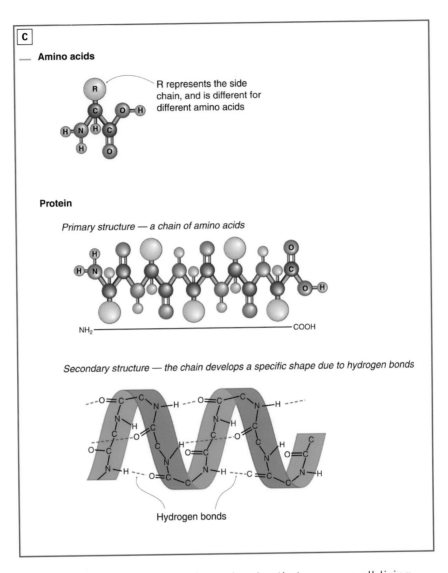

Figure 1.2 Biochemicals are the molecules that compose all living organisms. They can be divided into four categories, three of which are shown here: carbohydrates, fats, proteins, and nucleic acids. Agricultural biotechnology makes use of these molecules to make consumer products or to improve animals and crops.

(continued from page 5)

sheets of a protein called **keratin**. Proteins called **enzymes** carry out a variety of jobs for cells. Their main job is to perform the chemical reactions that run an organism's metabolism. Enzymes have thousands of uses in everyday life. They are commonly used in making certain foods and household substances. Proteins called **antibodies** fight disease and others called **storage proteins** act as reserves for amino acids. Proteins are unique because they are programmed by an organism's **genetic material**. Early advances in agricultural biotechnology have led to the commercial production of many economically important enzymes. These enzymes are used as cleaning agents and in manufacturing many types of chemicals.

Nucleic acids are a complex group of chemicals that have two primary functions in organisms. Simple nucleic acids called **nucleotides** take the energy from food and transfer it to the enzymes that control metabolism and other cell functions. Some simple nucleic acids use their energy transferring function as a way to signal cells to perform particular tasks. The other type of nucleic acid is made out of chains of nucleotides; these are called **compound nucleic acids**. These compound nucleic acids act as the genetic material for living organisms. The nucleic acid called **deoxyribonucleic acid** (**DNA**) is the chemical information making up the genetic material of most organisms. It programs the proteins that compose and run cells and tissues. **RNA** (**ribonucleic acid**) comes in many forms. RNA uses DNA to build proteins out of amino acids. Compound nucleic acids work the same way in all organisms. Thus, it is possible for scientists to take genetic material from one organism and, with some tweaking, place it into another. Scientists use this technique in agricultural biotechnology to produce new types of animals and plants.

Agricultural biotechnology is applied in two ways. The first application uses biochemicals from plants and animals to help produce food and chemicals. For example, lactic acid released by certain bacteria assist with the manufacturing of cheese and yogurt. The foods produced through agricultural biotechnology can be used for human consumption or as feed for animals. Biochemicals can also be employed in a variety of ways to make household chemicals or to carry out industrial processes. Certain sugars are modified by biotechnology processes to make bio-degradable or non-toxic dyes and glues. The second application of agricultural biotechnology involves creating GMOs. Some GMOs are used as new types of foods.

Stop and Consider

Describe how the absence of modern biotechnology could affect the following aspects of a fast-food meal:
- Looking at the lunch menu.
- Eating a hamburger made without refrigeration.
- Eating fries made from potatoes grown without pest control technologies.
- Having a salad harvested without tractors.

WHAT IS MODERN INDUSTRY?

Modern industry is best defined as the use of technology to produce resources. Resources include everyday things such as building materials, cars, electricity, food, and even video games. Different types of industries are grouped together into categories called "sectors." For example, electricity and natural gas are produced by the utilities sector. A toaster is made by the manufactured goods sector. An industry is considered "modern" when it uses current technology to carry out its operations. Today, an industry that runs without computers would be called "traditional" rather than "modern." Traditional industries usually involve a lot of human labor and require little technology. Many small businesses operate this way. It is also common for traditional industries to produce fewer resources over a period of time.

In 19th century Europe, the need for industries grew as cities became larger and fewer people performed agricultural jobs. Also, the need for highly efficient industries developed as the population expanded. People living in cities found little desire and ability to grow their own foods and make their own products. After all, people were spending much time performing jobs not related to agriculture. Manufacturing items for large urban populations is not a recent development. The ceramics, metal, stone, and wood used in building were manufactured in large amounts as far back as 5000 B.C. At the time, people improved the available technology to increase their productivity and reduce their costs. The first household items were manufactured by small industries around A.D. 600. Utensils and decorations made of brass, bronze, lead, silver, and tin were the most common items made then. Agriculture also became industrialized around this time, as farms became bigger and produced food for larger numbers of people. More efficient plows and harnesses made it easier to cultivate larger fields of crops. Specialized farming started around A.D. 500 to 700. The first silk-worm farm appeared during this period, reducing the need to harvest silk from silkworm caterpillars living in the forests.

Between A.D. 700 and 1000, most industrial growth focused on agriculture and large-scale food production. Clothing and household items then flourished between A.D. 1000 and 1200. High-tech innovations of the time included windmills for pumping water into neighborhoods and large looms for weaving fabric. By around A.D. 1300, the invention of blast furnaces and the development of paper production technology led to a great demand for larger and faster manufacturing. Modern industry did not reach its current potential until the discovery of fossil fuels such as coal and petroleum. People learned that they could replace animal and human labor with machines fueled by coal or oil. This made it more efficient to produce items for human survival. From this discovery, the industrial revolution was born in Europe around A.D. 1600. Today, a modern industry is one that uses machines and is controlled by computers.

WHAT IS INDUSTRIAL BIOTECHNOLOGY?

Industrial biotechnology is not easy to define. It describes many applications of biotechnology. Every type of industry has a biotechnology component. Even electrical energy production may be supplemented or replaced by industrial biotechnology processes. Some biotechnology industries use modern industrial processes to produce materials originally made by organisms. For example, an oily substance called glycerine that is found in many hand lotions was at one time collected from yeast. Now, it is made using chemical

What a Web We Weave!

It is safe to assume that if you came across a spider web you would conclude that a spider wove it—unless you believe that Spider-Man™ truly exists, that is. Thanks to recent advances in agricultural biotechnology, however, there are now other sources of spider webs. In 2001, a German scientist named Udo Conrad produced a genetically modified plant that made spider silk protein. He did this by first making a copy of a spider silk gene. Silk is a protein programmed by one or more genes. The gene was then placed into test plants that serve as models for plant genetic engineering studies. As the plants grew, they started producing large amounts of spider silk protein in their leaves and stems. The most successful part of the experiment was being able to collect the spider silk from the plants without any difficulty. Conrad tried this in plants after learning that he could get bacteria and yeast to produce silk from caterpillars and spiders. But why would a scientist want to make large amounts of spider web silk in the laboratory? Spider web silk is used in the production of special medical fabrics and bulletproof materials. Currently, it is very expensive to obtain spider web silk. Conrad is on the way to developing an inexpensive way of producing large volumes of the silk. It is hoped that plant cells containing the spider silk gene can be grown in large industrial vats. In a similar study completed in 2002, researchers at Nexia Biotechnologies in Massachusetts were able to get silk from cow and hamster cells grown in a laboratory. Again, this technique can produce valuable fibers used in surgical sutures and dental cements.

reactions that convert other molecules into glycerol. Other biotechnology industries use the organism as the technology to make various products. Many biotechnology industries focus on modifying organisms to improve the productivity of another industry. For example, the military uses genetically enhanced plants to assist with the breakdown of explosives polluting soil and water.

Stop and Consider

What would be the positive and negative consequences of giving up modern technology while trying to live and work in a city today?

The first biotechnology experiments were carried out between 6000 B.C. and A.D. 1700, when people selectively bred agricultural animals and plants for beneficial characteristics, in a process called **selective breeding**. They achieved this by continually breeding organisms with similar features so the whole population contanined those characteristics. Animals and plants with undesireable features were not permitted to breed which led to a loss of those undesirable characteristics. Many of these **traits** improved food production in the same way that advances in manufacturing technology improved industrial manufacturing. For example, strong, meaty cattle were bread with other strong, meaty cattle to produce strong and healthy offpring. Weak cows were not permitted to breed, and thus fewer weak cattle were produced. Another early type of biotechnology was **fermentation**—a process in which microorganisms convert sugars to alcohol—to make seasonings and beverages such as wine and beer. People recognized long ago that bacteria and **fungi** produced alcohol and flavors when grown under certain conditions.

Most advances in industrial biotechnology were driven by new discoveries in biology. A better understanding of organisms provided scientists with ways to manufacture new types of products. It also gave scientists novel ways to use organisms to perform jobs that were normally accomplished by chemical manufacturing or by humans. Organisms were developed that produced useful chemicals more simply and more pure than traditional chemical manufacturing techniques. Plus, the organisms can produce large volumes of chemical using fewer people to operate the processs.

The discovery of the structure of DNA in 1953 paved the way for industrial biotechnology (Figure 1.3). It provided the basis for understanding how organisms function. The discovery of the **gene** function in the 1960s made possible the first genetic engineering research in 1973. Eventually, modern industrial practices incorporated modern genetics to create industrial biotechnology. Today, industrial biotechnology is one of the fastest growing industries in the world.

Industrial biotechnology overlaps with agricultural, environmental, and pharmaceutical (medical) biotechnology. As described earlier, agricultural biotechnology involves the use and modification of organisms to produce food. Environmental biotechnology uses organisms to clean the environment. Pharmaceutical biotechnology involves the discovery and production of drugs for animals and humans. Industrial biotechnology works with the other types of biotechnology to provide a variety of commodities and services. Many of the ingredients found in today's foods were made using industrial biotechnology. Some form of industrial biotechnology is used to make one or more components of almost every common item we use every day.

Stop and Consider

Think of some ways that industrial biotechnology can be used to address the following contemporary needs:
- The shrinking supply of fossil fuels.
- The scarcity of vaccines during disease outbreaks.
- The need to monitor a person's heart from inside the body during his or her daily routine.
- A clean way to manufacture chemicals.

Figure 1.3 The discovery of DNA structure by James Watson and Francis Crick in 1953 paved the way for modern genetics. Pictured here is James Watson looking over the DNA "double helix" model built from research data. Further research illustrating the role of gene function led to the diverse science of biotechnology.

CONNECTIONS

Agriculture is one of the oldest applications of human observation of nature. It predates Greek science by at least 9,000 years. Ancient people in Asia and the Middle East were domesticating animals and plants even before there was a rudimentary understanding of genetics and inheritance. Agriculture developed when societies abandoned a wandering lifestyle and settled into villages that grew into cities. The formation of cities helped human populations flourish, thus providing a greater need for food. People devised selective breeding to produce animals and plants that provided abundant food. Selective breeding practices remained virtually unchanged until the discovery of modern genetics. The new science of genetics provided people with precision ways of producing large amounts of economically important animals and plants having desirable characteristics. Starting in the 1970s, the biotechnology technique called genetic engineering began replacing selective breeding. It provided quicker results and permitted scientists with a way to add or subject particular characteristics. Thus was born the science of agricultural biotechnology.

FOR MORE INFORMATION

For more information about the concepts discussed in this chapter, search the Web using the following keywords:

Biotechnology education, Biotechnology history, Biotechnology information, Genetic engineering, Genetically modified organism, Selective breeding, Fermentation, DNA

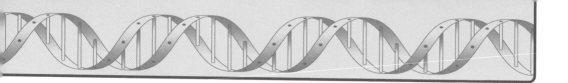

2

Agriculture Yesterday and Today

A BRIEF HISTORY OF AGRICULTURE

Agriculture is one of civilization's oldest occupations. It was central to the development of cities and remains a prominent part of almost every culture. Agriculture was the first of the "Technological Revolutions" that made up the Industrial Revolution that began in Europe in the 1600s. The term **agriculture** is best defined as the organized growing and management of animals and plants for commerce. Commerce is the production and sale of goods— in the case of agriculture, of food and other products made from plants and animals. Other products include a variety of everyday things. Any wood found around the house, for instance, is likely to have come from trees grown for that purpose. The same holds true for anything made out of paper. The glue used for holding wooden furniture together contains starch and other biochemicals derived from plants. Likewise, molecules such as carbohydrates and proteins from animals go into clothing, adhesives, makeup, and shampoo.

The first agricultural activity goes back to about 9000 B.C. when people started settling large cities in northern Africa and Asia. Little is known about this early agriculture because little was recorded about it in those days. Any recorded history of agricultural practices is difficult to decipher or was destroyed during invasions and war. Much of what is known was gathered from archaeological studies. Archaeologists (people who study early cultures) and anthropologists (people who study human societies) have found ancient remains of agricultural animal bones, cooking utensils, crop seeds, and farm tools. Some cultures still embody these early agricultural lifestyles (Figure 2.1).

Advances in agriculture went hand-in-hand with the development of other technologies. For instance the invention of the car led to the creation of the first tractor. Agriculture permitted civilizations to grow and prosper. It gave many people the ability to pursue other endeavors besides producing food. Skills and trades expanded as a smaller number of people were able to provide food for others in the community. People now had time to take on new tasks or to concentrate on perfecting their skills at specialized tasks. Some became skilled craftspeople, able to shape wood and metal for practical purposes. For example, around 6000 B.C., people started to perfect the use of copper. This might not have happened if the people who discovered copper's properties had been busy gathering food or tending farms to survive. The skills and trades developed by people who did not work on farms served two purposes in early societies. They provided a means of economic exchange to purchase food and clothing materials from farmers. They also provided the basis for many inventions that improved agricultural practices. For example,

Figure 2.1 Indigenous cultures of Africa, Asia, Lapland, Russia, and South America still carry out pre-agricultural lifestyles. They predominantly gather food and hunt for their family's resources. Some, as shown in the top photograph, maintain herds of animals for clothing and food. Others, as shown in the bottom photograph, have small family farms growing local plants for fruits, roots, and seeds.

people with mechanical skills improved farm machinery and food processing. The invention of air conditioning not only helped cool homes but it provided a means of effectively shipping and storing foods.

Agriculture today follows the same philosophy as 10,000 years ago: people want to grow as much of what they need while using the least amount of human effort. The main distinction between ancient and modern agriculture is the degree to which technology is used in farming. Agriculture has gone through four technological eras since 9000 B.C., characterized by the type of energy that drove the technology. The earliest era, spanning from 9000 B.C. to A.D. 600, is called the Biological Energy Sources Era. It was the longest period of agriculture and was able to feed the steadily growing world population. During this period animal and human labor provided the energy for harvesting, planting, and plowing. The next period was the Inanimate Energy Sources Era, which started in A.D. 600 and ended in the 1600s. Inanimate energy refers to the machinery that replaced the animals used to operate equipment such as plows. The agricultural techniques of this period were practiced similarly all over the world in countries with large urban areas. Throughout much of the developed world, this was seen as the use of simple machines, mills, and pumps driven by wind and water energy. Many archaeologists and anthropologists believe that early travelers who traded goods between Africa, Asia, and Europe told tales of agricultural practices in each region they visited. People borrowed the best agricultural practices of other cultures through migration and trade. The third period is called the Fossil Fuel Energy Source Era. It began in the A.D. 1600s, corresponding with the first use of coal and petroleum. The fourth period of agriculture is currently displacing the Fossil Fuel Energy Source Era. It is the Biotechnology Energy Source Era. This new era started in the 1980s and is still developing. It is reducing the need for other energy sources by relying on biotechnology to drive agricultural technology.

Stop and Consider

Imagine that you wanted to spend a week trying to live without agricultural products. How would you have to change your lifestyle to adapt to life without agriculture? What would you have to do to feed yourself? What would you have to do to clothe yourself? Would you be able to meet all your needs if you carried this out for a year?

Agriculture Then and Now

Civilization in industrialized nations would not be where it is today were it not for developments during the Biological Energy Sources Era. Cultures that have not adopted practices for cultivating large fields of food live predominantly as hunters and gatherers, maintaining small family farms. These small farms are used to grow local plants for fruits, roots, and seeds. Humans and animals fueled the technology in the Biological Energy Sources Era. During the early part of this era, farms served small villages made up of several families. These farms produced large fields of local plants and animals and provided more food than could be obtained through traditional food gathering and hunting methods. Not all families were involved in farming during the Biological Energy Source Era. Some made crafts, others hunted, and some conducted trade with other villages.

Life on a village farm during the Biological Energy Sources Era involved a great deal of human labor. The whole family, along with farmworkers hired to help the family, cared for the animals and tended the land. Some farms were tended by groups of families. In other areas, local governments organized the farms. Farming was aided by early attempts at animal and plant **domestication.** The regular use of domesticated animals and plants in farming operations began in the Middle East and North Africa in about 7000 B.C. In 6000 B.C., this practice spread to eastern and southern Europe. The strategy was then carried into central Europe by 4500 B.C. Chinese farmers started growing fields of domesticated crops in 5500 B.C. Trade and wars among various regions between 3500 and 500 B.C. further spread this practice to most of the cultures in Asia, northern Africa, Europe, and the Middle East, as soldiers brought news of the new technology home. Isolated from the rest of the world, the indigenous people of America domesticated corn in Mexico around

Taking the Bite out of Disease

Treating diseases in agricultural animals was a difficult task before the development of agricultural biotechnology. Chicken, cows, and pigs are plagued by dozens of diseases that harm them, other animals, and humans. People raising agricultural animals in tropical countries are at a considerable disadvantage, because of the great number of diseases found in those regions. This is becoming a global concern because an increasing proportion of chicken and cattle products are produced and shipped from these nations. Medicines and vaccines must be given to treat diseases in agricultural animals. These treatments can be expensive and they sometimes affect the quality of the products that can be produced from the animals receiving them. There are also concerns that regular use of certain drugs can produce diseases that resist further management of the disease. The simplest way to control diseases in agricultural animals is by preventing the diseases from occurring, although this strategy is not feasible for animals raised in large fields or animals bred in tropical nations. Many strategies that are used to prevent diseases in agricultural animals introduce hazardous pesticides into the environment. These pesticides can be taken in by the animals and passed along to people in the products made from these animals. A group of scientists at the Universidad del Valle de Guatemala are using biotechnology to develop a new disease prevention strategy. They are working on two ways to keep biting insects from spreading diseases to animals and humans. One strategy involves producing genetically engineered male insects that produce offspring that die early. These males are released into the environment to breed with females, which reduces the population of insects to a safe level. The other strategy involves the introduction of genetically modified disease organisms or pathogens into the biting insects. These altered disease organisms do not cause disease. They are spread from the insects to the animals and then transmitted to insects carrying dangerous pathogens. The altered organisms then displace the dangerous ones, thus reducing the spread of disease.

5000 B.C. We do not know if they learned domestication on their own or carried the knowledge with them before settling in the region.

Why was domestication such a favorable practice in agriculture? First, it permitted people to select plants and animals that were easy to grow and were good sources of food. People produced domesticated animals using a technique called **selective breeding**. They knew that breeding animals and plants with certain characteristics produced populations where more of the offspring had the desirable traits. Animals and plants without desirable traits were discarded, or not allowed to breed. Second, domestication allowed people to replace human power with animal power (Figure 2.2). The first wooden plows, developed around 4000 B.C., were designed to be pulled or pushed by people. People learned to breed cattle, donkeys, horses, and other animals that could do work around the farm. Dogs were bred to herd and protect the domesticated animals being raised for clothing and food. Animal-driven agriculture was improved by the invention of wheeled vehicles in 3200 B.C, which permitted the development of carts for transporting large amounts of food. It also helped lead to the invention of plows that were easier to pull.

The Inanimate Energy Sources Era gradually began to succeed the Biological Energy Sources Era in most countries by 1600 B.C. *Inanimate* means "not living;" the Inanimate Era involved the use of nonliving things to provide the energy. The first evidence of this period occurred in Iran around A.D. 600 with the creation of the windmill (Figure 2.3). Windmills were used to pump **irrigation** water and operate simple machines for preparing food. The irrigation water was originally intended to water crops, eliminating the dependence on rainfall. The availability of water was a major problem for early agriculture. Irrigation provided some protection against the unpredictability of the weather that brought rain during the growing seasons. It permitted people to divert floodwater away from crops and allowed them to get water to plants when rain was not available. Some of the water was also taken for domesticated animals to drink. Energy

Figure 2.2 The Biological Energy Sources Era of agriculture relied on the work of humans and animals to do the farming. This era began by using human power and ended with using animals to drive plows and light machinery, as shown in the top photograph. The Fossil Fuel Energy Source Era of agriculture is most noted for bringing about the invention of gasoline powered farm machinery, as shown in the bottom photograph.

Figure 2.3 Windmills, such as the one shown here, heralded the Inanimate Energy Sources Era of agriculture. They were used predominantly for crop irrigation, but also provided the energy to run simple machines for making food.

from wind power drove milling machines, which helped speed up food production. This, in turn, helped increase trade and produced a greater demand for crops. The Inanimate Energy Sources Era is noted for expanding agriculture into drier areas. Previously, most agriculture was done near water. It was common to see farms along the floodplains of rivers.

The period of agriculture most familiar to people today is the Fossil Fuel Energy Source Era. This period began with the invention of the mechanical seed drill in 1701. The seed drill was a simple machine that automatically planted seeds. Its invention led to the development of many other machines that helped replace animal-powered carts and plows. Most of this new technology was powered by burning coal that ran steam engines. Coal was used for melting metal by the Chinese in 10,000 B.C. However, it was not used to run machinery until the late 1600s. Steam-driven tractors were introduced in 1750 and were common by 1904. Next came the first practical gasoline engine, invented by J.J.E. Lenoir in 1860. Gasoline-engine tractors and farm equipment replaced steam-driven machinery by the 1920s. The improvement of trucks during World War I (1914–1918) inspired the first gasoline-powered farm equipment (Figure 2.4). Energy from fossil fuels also aided transportation and food processing. It fueled the barges, trains, and trucks moving the food throughout the country. Plus, fuel was burned for the machinery and refrigeration needed for food manu-facturing, packaging, and storage. This period significantly reduced the need for human labor on the farm. A single piece of farm equip-ment did the work of dozens of people. The number and size of farms also decreased during this era because less area was needed to produce large amounts of food. Agriculture was now consigned to rural areas. Later in this era cities did not need food to be grown nearby, because refrigeration and transportation technologies made

Stop and Consider

Many scientific discoveries were made well before many modern devices were invented. How do fossil fuels make it possible to carry out more types of scientific research? Do you think it would have been possible for the Biotechnology Energy Source Era of agriculture to take place without the development of fossil fuel energy?

Figure 2.4 Steam energy and electricity also played important roles during the Fossil Fuel Energy Source Era. Steam powered tractors allowed for faster and more efficient harvesting of crops. Steam energy and electricity also permitted the rapid long-distance transportation and refrigeration needed for efficient food distribution.

it possible to ship perishable commodities long distances. Airplanes and large ships made it possible to import crops that could not be grown locally. Also during this period, wind energy irrigation systems were replaced by electrical pumps used to move the water. Electricity is still predominantly produced using fossil fuels today.

Inventions of the Fossil Fuel Energy Source Era

Major inventions during the Fossil Fuel Energy Source Era include the following:

- Cotton gin by Eli Whitney (1794): Permitted automated cotton farming.

- Steel plow with interchangeable parts by Charles Newbold (1797): Made plows easily adaptable to engine-powered farm machinery.

- Automated food canning (1819): Facilitated the storage and transport of food products. Food could be overproduced without spoiling or going to waste.

- McCormick reaper (1834): Allowed the efficient harvesting of crops.

- Steel blade plows by John Lane (1834) and John Deere (1837): Aided crop production.

- Mowing machine by Edwin Budding (1844): Easily modified for harvesting crops and maintaining pastures.

- Steam tractor by Charles Deitz (1868): Replaced the need for plow animals and made better use of earlier farm technology such as harvesters and plows.

- Gas tractors first made by Charter Gasoline Engine Company of Sterling, Illinois (1910): Smaller, safer, and more efficient than steam tractors because they were lighter and did not explode.

- Prairie combine by Hiram Moore (1918): Opened agriculture to areas not normally favorable to farming because it was able to harvest crops and even separate the edible parts of the food from the waste.

- All-purpose rubber tires (1930): Improved the performance of farm machinery by making them lighter and able to roll more easily.

- Industrial fertilizers (1950): Less expensive and more effective than the earlier organic fertilizers made from animal and plant wastes. However, their overuse ultimately led to serious water pollution problems by the 1960s.

- Energy-efficient farm machinery and reduce tillage practices (1989): Reduced the energy needed to conduct agricultural operations, thus lowering the cost of food production and reducing damage to agricultural land. Less fuel was needed to run the new farm equipment. Plus, agricultural researchers developed ways for farmers to reduce the number of times they had to use the machinery to treat the soil.

The Biotechnology Energy Source Era did not replace the Fossil Fuel Energy Source Era, but rather supplemented it in much the same way that the Inanimate Energy Source Era assisted the Biological Energy Source Era. Similarly, energy from the metabolism of agricultural genetically modified organisms drives the Biotechnology Energy Source Era. The hallmark of this era was the first successful genetic engineering trials performed by Stanley Cohen & Herbert Boyer in 1973. They introduced various animal genes into bacteria. From this point forward, scientists were interested in producing commercially important organisms. It provided hope for replacing the slow and inaccurate selective breeding strategies used for thousands of years. Selective breeding took many years to produce desirable organisms. Genetic engineering performed the same task in much less time. This era is streamlining agricultural practices by producing crops and animals that require less energy and fewer resources to produce. The scientists influencing the Biotechnology Energy Source Era are looking into ways for producing power using the metabolism of genetically modified organisms. The discoveries of this era are discussed in Chapters 3 and 4 of this book.

CONNECTIONS

Human energy fueled the first agricultural practices and introduced the Biological Energy Sources Era. People pushed or pulled the plows needed to cultivate the soil and plant crop seeds. Animals were manually fed, milked, and slaughtered for food. This was not an effective way to carry out agriculture. Many people were needed to produce food for a small city or a village. Human energy gave way to the animal derived energy. Plows and early farm machinery were driven by animals, making it possible for less people to grow more food. This Biological Energy Sources Era was in turn replaced in the 1600s by inanimate energy sources such as wood and fossil fuels. These new energy sources were favorable for running many types of inventions that made agriculture more efficient. Modern fuel-powered tractors replaced the labor of dozens of humans and animals.

A modern Biotechnology Energy Source Era came into existence with the advent of genetic engineering. Scientists began developing cell cultures capable of producing a wide variety of agricultural and consumer chemicals and materials. Many commercial chemicals were once made by extracting the chemical from cultivated or collected animals and plants. Now, the same products are made in large quantities by vats of genetically modified cells grown relatively inexpensively. Plus, the products can be collected without having to kill the cells. Scientists are currently looking at using biotechnology as an energy source. Initial studies are showing that cells can be grown under certain conditions so that their metabolism can produce electrical energy. This electricity can be the fuel to run agricultural operations and even everyday aspects of life.

FOR MORE INFORMATION

For more information about the concepts discussed in this chapter, search the Web using the following keywords:

Agriculture, Agriculture history, Ancient farming, Energy history, Industrial Revolution, Modern agriculture

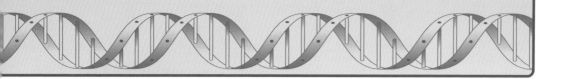

3

Biotechnology in Crop Production

The search for provisions to feed rapidly growing populations drove humans from Africa to Asia, Europe, and the Middle East. People settling in these new lands had to adapt to the new foods that they gathered and hunted. Eventually, as they formed large settlements, they set up farms to grow food. People discovered that farming the local plants was the most effective way to feed large populations. They also learned that certain plants grew better than others, and selectively cultivated these plants. This discovery, called selective breeding, heralded the beginning of modern agriculture. Through selective breeding, people were able to develop crops that produced more seeds, larger roots, tastier leaves, and thicker tubers (underground stems). They also learned how to select crops that survived better, thus providing a more consistent supply of food.

As people moved into new regions of the world, they brought with them the plants they had grown in their homelands.

Unfortunately, these plants often failed to grow well in the new locations. Thus, one aspect of agriculture focused on selective breeding to adapt these plants to new growing conditions. This led to an agricultural practice called **monoculture**. Monoculture is the selective breeding of large amounts of a single type of agricultural animal and plant. Sometimes, monoculture was not successful at improving crop yield (the amount of usable food). This forced people to develop new practices that aided the growth of these crops. People worked on improving fertilizers, irrigation, and soil treatment, starting around 4000 B.C.

Rapid industrialization and the boom of restaurant dining after the 1950s encouraged a greater desire for crop consistency (Figure 3.1). People in industrialized nations wanted to have consistent food quality. Plus, national restaurant chains wanted to provide the same taste to the meals served throughout the country. Manufacturers who used crop products needed uniform raw materials for the items they were producing. Stiff competition within and between countries made it necessary for manufacturers to have access to supplies of high-quality material. Clothing manufactures needed cotton fibers that had the same feel and dye-retention properties to ensure consistent quality for each garment made. Chemical companies that used agricultural products as raw material had contractual obligations to make consistent products. Government policies over manufacturing processing made product consistency a prority for consumer safety and satisfaction. Thus companies could

Stop and Consider

How would your life be affected if the following agricultural products had little consistency of quality: wheat, cotton, potatoes? How would your life be affected if the following agricultural products could not be provided regularly throughout the year, and from one year to another: corn, tomatoes, apples?

Figure 3.1 The boom of restaurant dining after the 1950s encouraged a greater desire for crop consistency. People wanted restaurant meals that would taste the same with each visit. They also expected high quality food every time. Today, scientists are able to meet the growing demand for consistently high quality crops through the production of genetically modified or bio-engineered crops.

not sell different quality items using the same product names and claims. Consumer demand also compelled food manufacturers to strive for consistency in the quality of the animals and plants. People wanted assurance that the foods they purchased at grocery stores and

number of new crop varieties. Scientists were hampered by the limitations of selective breeding until the development of **recombinant DNA technology** in 1972. Recombinant DNA technology gave the hope of being able to rapidly develop highly desirable crops. Using recombinant DNA technology scientists are able to insert DNA with desirable traits into the cells of another organism. As a result the organism is able to take on the new traits and pass them along to its offspring. Initially, it appeared that recombinant DNA technology would not be useful for plant breeding. It had only been performed successfully on bacteria, which have simple DNA that is relatively easy to manipulate. Not enough was known about plant genes to be able to select traits for recombinant DNA experimentation. It was not until the 1980s that recombinant DNA technology was possible in plants. Another problem was how to get the new DNA into a majority of the plant's cells. Unlike bacteria, which are single-celled, plants are composed of millions of cells.

Recombinant DNA technology is a way of producing organisms with desire traits by inserting genes into an organism's cells. In bacteria, the technique involves inserting genes into the **genome** of a bacterial cell (Figure 3.3). Genome refers to the complete DNA information of an organism. This is more difficult to do in the complex cells found in animals and plants. In plants, the added DNA is placed into the cell using an artificial **chromosome** called a **transfection vector**. The tranfection vector is designed in such a way that the cell receiving it uses the inserted genes in a specific manner so that the characteristic turns on in specific plant parts or only under certain conditions. The DNA added during recombinant DNA technology can come from a related organism. **Transgenic** recombinants receive DNA from an unrelated organism. Transgenic means to transfer genes from one type of organism to another. For instance, certain types of crops are given bacterial genes that produce chemicals that kill certain insects.

(continued on page 40)

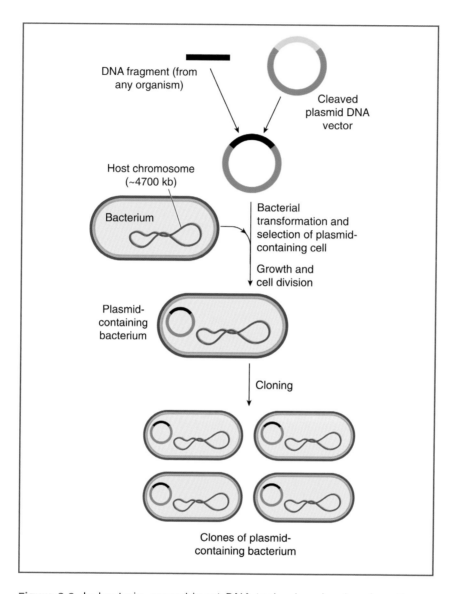

Figure 3.3 In bacteria, recombinant DNA technology involves inserting genes into the genome or chromosome of a bacterial cell. The bacteria then use the gene as if it is part of the normal DNA. These new characteristics are passed along through the next generations of bacteria as they undergo reproduction.

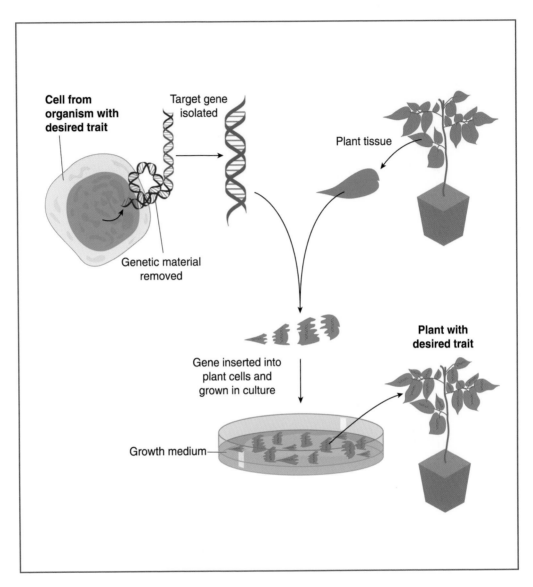

Figure 3.4 Illustrated here is the most common way scientists produce recombinant plants. First, scientists collect cells from an organism containing the desired characteristic. Then, they isolate the gene for the desired characteristic and insert it into the new organism. Then they grow the organism in the lab to see if it has the desired characteristics.

(continued from page 37)

Recombinant DNA technology is not something that can be carried out in just anybody's kitchen. It requires precise conditions to ensure that the new DNA works properly. The following steps outline the most common method scientists use to produce recombinant plants (Figure 3.4):

1. Identify the gene that controls the desired trait.

2. Remove the gene using enzymes.

3. Insert the gene into a small piece of DNA called a cloning vector.

4. Place the cloning vector into bacterial or yeast cells. The cloning vector permits bacteria or yeast to replicate the gene.

5. Use the bacteria or yeast to make multiple copies of the vector (cloning).

6. Remove the copies (clones) and insert them into a new vector.

7. Insert the vector into plant cells grown in culture.

8. Test the cells to determine if the genes on the vector are placed in the cell properly and are working the way they should. The cells are now **transfected.**

9. Place the transfected cells into a special culture that enables them to grow into a whole new plant made of genetically altered cells.

10. Test the new plants by growing them in a greenhouse to see if they have the desired traits.

11. Breed the plants to see if they pass the desired traits to their offspring.

12. Grow the plants on farms to see if they perform as expected.

Stop and Consider

What characteristics could you envision adding to the following plants to create new uses for them: apples, corn, cotton, peanuts, and potatoes?

There are many challenges to introducing new genes into an organism. Getting the genes to work properly is a major concern for scientists producing a transgenic organism. Scientists have to ensure that the gene is properly placed so that the cell will find it. At the same time, the gene must be placed in the cells so it does not interfere with the function of the genes already in the organism's genome. This is usually achieved by packaging the new gene as a separate, distinct body called a **plasmid**. This can also be accomplished by inserting the new gene into a "safe" location on one of the organism's chromosomes—that is, a location where there are no functional genes whose function could be disrupted. Once inserted into the cell, the gene must be able to turn on and off at the appropriate times so that it achieves an acceptable degree of **expression**. It is also essential that the gene be activated where it produces value in the transgenic organism. For example, some genes need to be expressed in roots and not in leaves. The genes must, therefore, be inserted with additional DNA sequences that ensure the DNA produces the desired characteristic. Once expression is confirmed, the scientists must ensure that the new trait does not harm the organism or display any potential of harming other plants and animals.

Traditional selective breeding can take several years to produce a uniform crop with the desired traits. It can take up to three years to breed new varieties of rapidly growing plants such as corn, and eight years for slow growing plants such as apples. Recombinant DNA technology permits more precision than selective breeding. Scientists can tailor plants by adding only the genes they want, while simultaneously excluding any undesirable characteristics. Selective breeding sometimes perpetuates the passage of unwelcome characteristics that decrease the quality of the crop. One significant unwelcome characteristic is the inadvertent loss of protective genes during selective breeding. In some plants, for example, the ability to resist drought and fight off pests has disappeared after years of selective breeding. This was discovered in the 1960s and 1970s when large fields of selectively bred cotton were lost to fungal diseases. Agricultural scientists believed that years of selective breeding accidentally bred away the genes that protected the ancestral plants from the fungi. Similar events happened in canola, potatoes, rice, and wheat.

Many precautions are taken to ensure that the genetically modified plants will not cause harm to animals and humans. They are tested for any possible toxins or compounds that can cause allergies. They are also tested to see if they may damage the local environment when released onto farms. To do this, small field tests are conducted to see if the crops escape to displace native plants in the area. They are also tested to see if the genes introduced from the plants are somehow transferred to wild plants. Most scientists add special genes that prevent the plants from getting out into the environment. For instance, a set of genes can be added that prevent the crop plant's pollen from successfully fertilizing wild plants. Sometimes genes are added that prevent the genetically altered crop from producing pollen. The passage of genes from one organism to another is called **horizontal gene transfer.** Horizontal gene transfer is most likely to occur when a gene passes from the pollen of genetically modified plants to related plants that are not genetically altered.

GENETICALLY MODIFIED ORGANISM (GMO) CROPS

Genetically modified agricultural plants (and animals, which will be discussed in Chapter 4) are not created merely because they are scientific novelties. Scientists are not knowingly creating and indiscriminately releasing monsters from their laboratories. These organisms are produced because they have beneficial characteristics that cannot be achieved through selective breeding.

Hunting Elusive Genes

Scientists with the U.S. Department of Agriculture (USDA) spend much of their time conducting research outside the United States. Groups of researchers travel the globe, collecting plant genes from everything from exotic crops to scrawny weeds. They are interested in finding genes for use in the production of new types of corn, cotton, potatoes, soybeans, and wheat. Why are scientists interested in going out of their way to add new genes to these crops? Years of practicing a type of selective breeding called monoculture have caused the accidental loss of certain genes from these crops. Many of these genes imparted protective properties that were not recognized as useful in the early days of agriculture. Monoculture focuses on growing a consistent field of crops that have a particular set of traits. Any variation from these traits was discouraged by breeding out the genes for the undesirable characteristics. Unfortunately, in the process, many plants lost traits that protected them against unfavorable conditions. The constant care and energy put into growing the plants sheltered the crops to the extent that they became genetically defenseless. Continuous pesticide applications since the 1940s eventually led to a renewed need for these traits, as diseases and pests became resistant to the pesticides. This left the plants vulnerable to attack. Additionally, traits that protected the plants from drought and infertile soil were also lost, making the plants susceptible to restricted farming practices mandated by the government. USDA researchers, therefore, have embarked on a worldwide search for the ancestors of the crop plants in the hopes that these ancestral plants still have the protective genes. Presumably, the ancestral forms of these plants need these genes to survive in their natural environment. So scientists travel to the Middle East in search of ancestral wheat, or to Central America, the home of corn and potato plants. If the valuable genes are found, they will be collected and placed into genetically altered cells and kept frozen in institutions called gene banks. Scientists will then be able to go to the gene banks to find genes that make hardier crops.

What are the major justifications for using genetically modified organisms (GMOs) in agriculture? First, scientists can develop organisms that meet the needs of farmers and consumers. Second, GMOs can be used to reduce the need for fertilizer and pesticides, thus reducing the amount of pollution produced by agricultural operations. GMOs also limit human exposure to agricultural chemicals that may make their way into food. Third, GMOs can be developed to grow under conditions that would not normally favor agriculture. Another reason to produce GMOs is to yield agricultural organisms that have higher nutritional value.

Any meal you eat today is likely to have at least one ingredient that has been produced through recombinant DNA technology (Figure 3.5). Some countries restrict the types of GMO crops that can be consumed by people. The governments feel that not everything is known about the safety of GMO foods. So, they limit the types of GMO foods that are consumed by people. Below are some of the GMO crops being grown and tested in various countries; some are still subject to regulations:

- Aspen trees: Contain a gene that overproduces a hormone responsible for paper fiber production.

- Beans: Contain genes that prevent insects from feeding on the pods and seeds.

- Canola: This type of mustard plant contains a gene that protects it from herbicides used to kill weeds. Others contain genes for producing economically important oils. Another type has genes for improving the vitamin E content of the plant.

- Cassava: Contains a gene that prevents poisonous cyanide from forming when it is ground up for making flour.

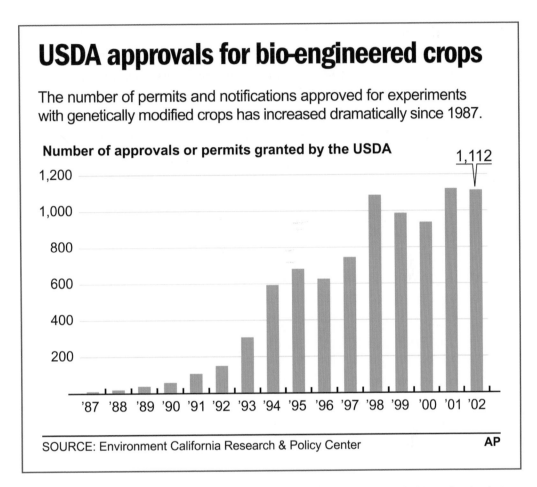

USDA approvals for bio-engineered crops

The number of permits and notifications approved for experiments with genetically modified crops has increased dramatically since 1987.

Number of approvals or permits granted by the USDA

1,112

SOURCE: Environment California Research & Policy Center   AP

Figure 3.5 Biotechnology is becoming more prevalent in agriculture. Many foods that you eat today are made from genetically modified organisms. This graph shows the rapid development of bio-engineered crops from 1987 through 2002.

- Coffee: Contains genes that turn off caffeine production (in plants used to make decaffeinated coffee).

- Corn: Contains a variety of genes for herbicide and insect resistance. Some corn has genes that stop toxic fungi from making corn products unsafe. Many genetically engineered corn varieties have genes that make the male parts sterile to prevent horizontal gene transmission.

• Cotton: Contains genes for herbicide and insect resistance.

• Papaya: Contains a gene that fights off plant viruses.

• Potato: Many varieties contain genes for herbicide and insect resistance. Others have been produced for novel properties such as unique colors or tastes.

• Rice: Contains genes that improve nutritional value. Scientists are testing two varities of rice which contain either the gene for increasing vitamin A or the gene for increasing iron (fortified rice).

• Soybean: Contain genes that protect the plant from herbicides used to kill weeds. Other soybeans contain genes for producing economically important oils.

• Squash: Contains a gene that fights off plant viruses.

• Sugarbeet: Contain genes that protect the plant from herbicides used to kill weeds.

• Tomato: One type has genes that protect the plant against insects. Another type has genes that increase the nutrients beta-carotene and lycopene believed to ward off cancer. One type has genes to prevent ripening prematurely.

Stop and Consider

What other crop products do you shop for that could benefit from some of the genes listed in the plants on the previous page?

CONNECTIONS

Any meal eaten in much of the world today is likely to have one ingredient produced by recombinant DNA technology. Some countries still restrict the types of GMO crops that can be consumed by people. Some of the major GMO crops being developed or grown for agricultural and industrial uses include beans, corn, and cotton.

So far, these GMOs have proven economically feasible. There is no evidence that they have caused harm to humans or the environment when grown as field plants. Traditional seed companies are continuing to invest research dollars into the development of GMOs that improve upon the characteristics of current crops. Many governments are encouraging biotechnology companies to set up operations in their countries or regions. Every year, the Biotechnologies Industry Organization hosts the BIO International Convention to review agricultural biotechnology innovations and encourage discussions between economic development representatives and leaders from successful biotechnology companies.

FOR MORE INFORMATION

For more information about the concepts discussed in this chapter, search the Web using the following keywords:

Biotechnology crops, Monoculture, Crop genomics, GMO crops, Hybrid crops, Transfection, Recombinant DNA technology, Horizontal gene transfer

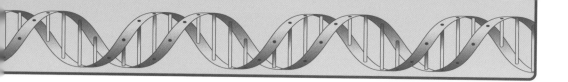

4

Biotechnology in Animal Agriculture

Animals have always played a role in human survival by being a primary source of clothing and food. Early hunting and gathering societies sought prey based on the quality of the animals' meat and fur. Like other hunting animals, people primarily selected prey that was easy to catch or trap. Birds, fish, rabbits, and rodents most likely formed much of the diets of early humans. These animals were not adequate for producing garments and shelters (for instance, tents and huts), however, so larger game such as antelope, bears, big cats, buffalo, deer, and elephants were hunted—despite the risk of injury or death.

It is believed that people started domesticating cats and dogs as pets over 10,000 years ago. Early civilizations used selective breeding to produce tame cats with a variety of aesthetic characteristics. Most famous are the Abyssinian and Egyptian cats seen in hieroglyphs and statues from ancient Middle Eastern tombs (Figure 4.1). The

mask unfavorable genes that appear in the population. Recessive desirable genes can lose the ability to produce the trait if covered up by dominant genes or blended with other recessive genes having different characteristics. Genetic lineages provided more accurate information than tracking bloodlines, although it did not significantly improve the outcomes of selective breeding. The practice still required coercing male animals to breed with females that had similar genetic characteristics to produce a large proportion of offspring with the desired characteristics.

Improvements in selective breeding came about in the 1980s as scientists developed laboratory techniques for identifying and locating genes. They were now able to determine whether a particular gene was in an organism under consideration for selective breeding. Now it was possible to perform a genetic analysis on the animals to identify all the known genes. Genomic research projects for mapping the genomes of cattle, chicken, horses, and pigs got under way in the mid-1990s. Incorporating genomic research with other breeding technologies made it possible to produce desirable varieties of animals in one generation. Genomic information was useful for breeders who carried out artificial insemination and *in vitro* fertilization on their animals. **Artificial insemination** involves

PRO or CON?

Biotechnology and the Pet Store

The development of GMO animals for agriculture opened the door for GMO pets. Scientists can now clone a favorite pet or produce novel pets with unusual characteristics such as the "GloFish," which is a fish that glows in the dark. What are the pros and cons of using genetic technology for producing new types of pets? What are the pros and cons of using genetic technology for cloning aging or dead pets?

collecting sperm from particular breeds of animal. The sperm was chosen because it had been confirmed to carry the genes for desired traits and lack genes for undesired characteristics. Breeding is accomplished by inserting tubes of sperm into the female animal's reproductive tract. *In vitro* **fertilization** (**IVF**) refers to fertilization "in glass." Selected sperm are mixed with selected eggs in a laboratory culture. The fertilized egg is then placed in the female animal, where the offspring with the desirable characteristics develops. Females carrying these offspring are called **surrogates** (Figure 4.2).

HOW HAS BIOTECHNOLOGY IMPROVED ANIMAL BREEDING?

Artificial insemination and IVF can only introduce characteristics that are already present in the particular animal's population. They cannot create new traits. The mid-1990s saw the introduction of genetic engineering strategies that were useful for animal breeding. Genetic engineering enabled scientists to manipulate genes or add genes from other organisms. Other biotechnology strategies permitted the production of uniform animal populations having little or no genetic variability.

Embryo splitting was the first strategy attempted for producing uniform animals with desirable characteristics. Scientists in the late 1970s were able to collect a cow **embryo** and artificially separate it into several parts that grew up into identical offspring, or clones. The process is similar to the natural twinning event that produces identical twins or triplets. Split embryos can be placed into surrogate mothers to produce a herd of uniform offspring. This expensive procedure is used primarily for specialty cattle and GMO animals.

Genetic engineering of animals lagged behind the original studies carried out on bacteria. As mentioned earlier this was due in part to the fact that animal DNA is much more complex than bacterial DNA. Until the early 1990s, it was not feasible to produce genetically modified (GM) agricultural animals. Genetic engineering is more difficult to perform in animals than in plants, largely because animal cells are more difficult to grow in a laboratory. Even today, it is difficult to grow or clone a whole animal from one cell, as can be done readily with plants. A whole plant can be grown from a group of cells placed in a laboratory culture. Animal cells require a delicate balance of hormones and nutrients that are not easy to maintain in laboratory cultures. At this time, egg cells and special cells called **stem cells** are the only cells readily able to generate a complete animal. It was through the extension of stem cell research that the first animal cloned from an adult cell—a sheep called Dolly—was produced in 1996 (Figure 4.3). The scientists cloning Dolly were able to get the DNA from a mature cell to initiate development of an egg into an embryo. This process is called **somatic cell cloning** and is the type of cloning often associated with genetic engineering. This is a complicated, difficult technology and is only rarely successful in animals. Adult somatic cells do not have the metabolism necessary to regenerate a whole organism. Unlike somatic cells, the contents of an egg cell contain enzymes and hormones that facilitate development into an embryo.

There are currently three strategies used for genetically engineering agricultural animals: **recombinant DNA** technology, **transgenic GMO** production, and **chimera** production. Recombinant DNA technology in animals involves precise conditions to ensure that the new DNA works properly in the animal. The following steps outline the most common method scientists use to produce recombinant animals for agriculture or research:

1. Find a gene for the desired trait.

2. Remove the gene using specific enzymes.

3. Modify the gene, if necessary.

4. Insert the gene into a cloning vector.

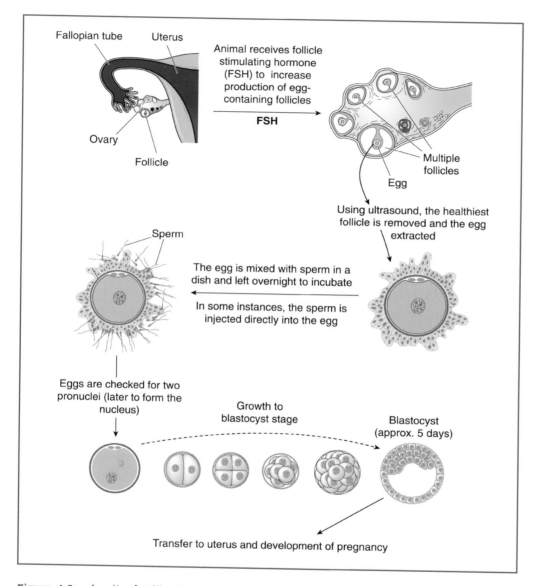

Figure 4.2a *In vitro* fertilization refers to fertilization "in glass" (in a tube or dish rather than in a living organism). Selected sperm are mixed with selected eggs in a laboratory culture. The fertilized egg is grown in culture until it proves to be healthy and shows the desired characteristics. It is then placed in female animals where the offspring grow with the desirable characteristics.

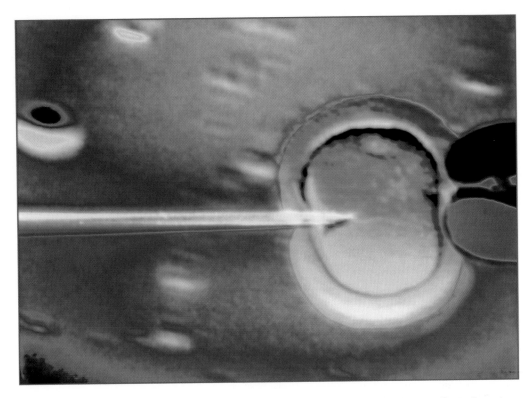

Figure 4.2b This photograph shows a researcher using a microscopic needle to insert desired genes into a fertilized egg. This egg will then be placed in a female animal where it grows into a young organism carrying the new traits.

5. Place the cloning vector into bacterial or yeast cells.

6. Use the bacteria or yeast to make multiple copies of the vector (cloning).

7. Remove the copies and insert them into a new vector.

8. Insert the vector into animal eggs grown in culture.

9. Test the eggs to determine if the genes on the vector are placed in the cell properly and are working the way they should. The cells are now transfected.

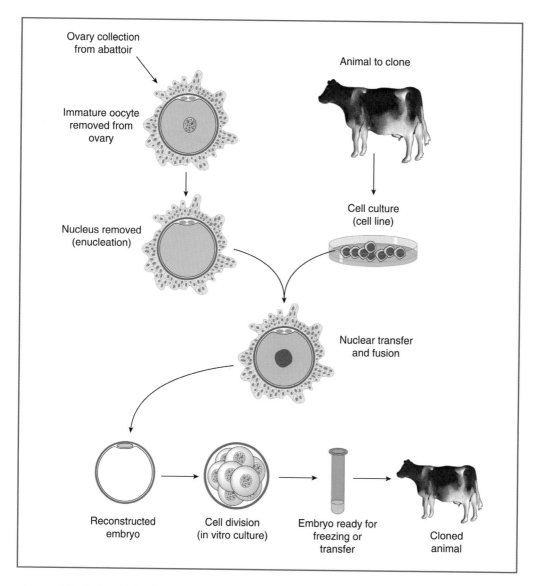

Figure 4.3 Animal cloning can be achieved by placing the genetic material of an animal into an egg that has had its DNA removed. In this diagram, the genetic material of a cow is used to produce a clone of that cow. The cow's genetic material is placed into an egg that is then grown in another cow, called the surrogate. This surrogate then gives birth to the clone.

10. Place the tranfected cells into a special culture that permits them to grow into an early embryo called a **blastula.**

11. Insert the blastula into a surrogate female.

12. Test the offspring to see if it possesses the desired trait.

13. Sometimes it is necessary to breed the animal to see if it passes the desired traits into the offspring.

14. Grow the animals on farms to see if they perform as expected.

Transgenic animals produced through the process of genetic modification are created in a similar manner to traditional recombinant DNA techniques. However, in transgenic animals, the genes inserted into the cells are derived from another organism. The new genes have to be placed on specific vectors that permit them to be expressed in certain cells under particular conditions.

Chimera production is an unusual technique that creates a blended animal that cannot produce offspring like itself. They are capable of producing egg and sperm representing each animal in the blend. The chimera gets its name from a mythical animal comprised of parts from several different animals. Chimeras were first used to understand animal development. Researchers wanted to see if the different cells could communicate with each other to "build" a single organism. They ultimately proved useful in agriculture, industry, and medicine. The following steps outline the most common way scientists produce chimeric animals for agriculture or research:

1. Collect embryonic cells from an organism expressing the desired traits.

2. Insert the cells into the developing embryo of a host animal.

3. Culture the host embryo, checking to see if the introduced cells are healthy.

4. Place the chimeric embryo into a surrogate mother.

5. Check the offspring to see if it has the desired characteristics.

The first chimeras were produced using another strategy. Scientists learned long ago that two embryos could fuse together if placed next to each other. This happens occasionally in animals that carry multiple offspring. Sometimes two embryos fuse forming parastic twins. This is in contrast to conjoined twins which is the incomplete separation of indentical twins that were forming from one egg. Fusion in the lab and in nature has two outcomes. The first outcome is that one embryo overgrows and swallows up the other. The second outcome produces a chimera: The two embryos fuse into one blended organism. Scientists in the United Kingdom were able to produce a chimera using sheep and goats. The resulting animals are nicknamed "Geeps." They vary in appearance with each fusion and, when fertile, produce offspring that are either pure goat or pure sheep. The gonads of "Geeps" retain their ability to produce the eggs or sperm of the goat and sheep.

GENETICALLY MODIFIED (GM) ANIMALS TODAY

GM agricultural animals are not as common as GM crops. Most GM animals are used in research, chemical manufacturing, and pharmaceuticals production. The use of GM animals for drug production is called **pharming**. The term pharming is a play on words meaning using farm animals to produce pharmaceuticals. Dozens of different types of GM rats are used for medical research. The introduction of genes that help fight or prevent infectious and genetic diseases is currently being investigated for many different agricultural animals, including cattle, chickens, pigs, and sheep.

Below are some of the GMO agricultural animals currently in use or under development:

- Cattle: Contain a modified gene that almost doubles muscle production, meaning more meat. Some are being tested with genes that make milk with either lower fat or higher protein content. Others are being researched to see if they can produce milk that contains vaccines against deadly human bacterial and viral diseases such as cholera.

- Chicken: Genes that enable chickens to produce eggs that are lower in cholesterol are currently in use. Genes that fight diseases spread by chickens are also being investigated.

- Fish: Several types of fish have been genetically modified for rapid growth, including carp, catfish, salmon, tilapia, and trout. Some salmon are given genes that help them survive better in the wild.

- Goats: Various genes involved in pharming are given to goats. The drugs can then be collected from the blood or milk. Scientists at Nexia in Canada are looking at this technique to produce human clotting factor treatments for helping hemophiliacs. Hemophiliacs have trouble clotting their blood because they are lacking critical blood factors.

- Insects: Research is under way to produce GM insects with high food value. The insects can be added to animal foods as a source of protein and vitamins.

- Pigs: A pig has been produced that expresses human surface **antigen** proteins. These surface antigens are important in transplant rejection. Transplanted organs are rejected when certain antigens do not match up with the person receiving the organ. This may permit physicians to use pig organs for human transplantation. Pigs containing modified genes that accelerate growth are also being grown. Research is being done to develop pigs that produce cow's milk. This is currently being done only for investigational purposes to see if it is possible to get one animal to produce the milk of another.

- Sheep: Genes that produce various proteins having medical value are added to sheep. The proteins can be collected from the sheep's blood or milk for pharming. Sheep with genes that accelerate growth are also being produced. Genes to improve wool production are being investigated.

Stop and Consider

Explain the benefits of producing animals that contain human genes. What types of characteristics do you feel should not be placed into animals? Also mention why certain traits should not be introduced into animals.

PRO or CON?

GMOs and Medicine

Biotechnology has allowed scientists to make new types of organisms that would not normally be found in nature. These novel organisms are not made for entertainment purposes. The new combination of traits imparts beneficial characteristics with commercial or medical value. However, it is not fully known if these new organisms pose any potential risks to human health. This technology for manipulating genes can also work on humans. What are the pros and cons of scientists being able to manipulate the genetics of a human? How do you feel about this?

CONNECTIONS

The first domesticated animals surprisingly were not bred for food. Cats and dogs were raised by ancient civilizations for companionship and for their hunting skills. People had pet cats and dogs around their houses for over 10,000 years. In those times, food was gathered by hunting animals such as birds, deer, fish, rabbits, and rodents. However, hunting did not provide all the meat needed to feed the large populations of people settling in cities around 6,000 B.C. It was not feasible for city dwellers to hunt, so they started keeping animals in large pens to have easier access to their food. This method of raising food soon became obsolete and people began using selective breeding to produce desirable animals that grew well and provided abundant meat or milk. By 4000 B.C., animals such as cattle, sheep, and goats were domesticated and raised for milk, meat, and fur.

Biotechnology made it possible to accelerate the breeding of a large variety of animals. The first biotechnology to be used in animal agriculture was artificial insemination, which made it easier to breed animals. This was followed by *in vitro* fertilization, making it possible to improve the reproductive success of the animals. It also allowed scientists to analyze the DNA and then split the embryos, in effect cloning the desirable animals. Scientists then developed the ability to modify the genes of animals including adding genes from one animal into another. This of course streamlined animal breeding and improved the precision adding desirable traits. Today, genetically modified farm animals are being evaluated for the production of medicines.

FOR MORE INFORMATION

For more information about the concepts discussed in this chapter, search the Web using the following keywords:

Dominant and recessive genes, *In vitro* **fertilization**, **Stem cells**, **Pharming**, **Somatic cell cloning**, **GMO animals**, **Livestock genomics**

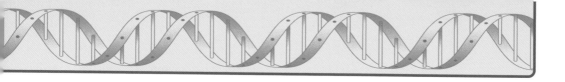

5

The Growth of Industry and Commerce

Since the early 1980s, biotechnology has contributed to the growth of worldwide industry and commerce. Some economists view biotechnology as the next technological revolution following the computer technology boom. Industry and commerce were natural directions for populations to take after they abandoned hunting and gathering in favor of forming communities built around agriculture. People saw more need to control their environment as they began to settle in a single area for many years. They had to ensure that they had adequate living conditions and resources for their growing populations. People also saw a need for trade with people from other places to bring in resources that were not available in their regions. Industry developed as a way for people to manufacture the commodities they needed to run their societies. Commerce developed as a means to obtain resources they could not collect or grow.

Biotechnology could not have developed without the concurrent growth of scientific knowledge and modern technology. Science provided the understanding of biochemistry and genetics that was essential to the application of molecular biology. Molecular biology is a relatively new discipline that grew from the fields of biochemistry and genetics, themselves relatively new sciences compared to chemisty and physics. Molecular biology was born from an integrated knowledge of traditional biology, chemistry, and physics. Traditional biology focused on classifying organisms and understanding major components of the body. Modern technology was the stimulus for using biotechnology to improve industry and commerce, as well as medicine, health, and politics. Modern biochemistry started in the 1800s with the detailed understanding of cellular **metabolism**. The term "cellular metabolism" refers to the chemical reactions cells use to obtain energy for staying alive. Modern genetics began with the discovery of DNA function in 1961. The Industrial Revolution of Europe saw the development of inventions that provided the technological means to mesh biochemistry and genetics into biotechnology applications. The instruments used for analyzing industrial chemicals were readily adapted for determining the characteristics of biological molecules such as DNA and proteins. Plus, many of the manufacturing machinery used in food production could be modified for culturing organisms that produce biotechnology products.

Every industrial and commercial sector since the Industrial Revolution began has been influenced to some extent by biotechnology innovations. The simplest of the biotechnology improvements supplement traditional technologies. For instance, the alcohol produced by the breakdown of farm wastes is used to supplement gasoline for automobiles and small engines. However, a growing number of biotechnology developments are replacing traditional inventions. The Industrial Revolution of the 1700s was born out of the desire to replace animal and human labor. The ability to harness fossil fuel energy became the driving force of the Industrial Revolution. Waterpower was one of the first energy sources people attempted to use to produce energy to run their machinery. This proved to be inconvenient because it had to be located near running water. So, other sources were investigated. Eventually, the energy produced from burning wood to operate machinery was replaced by the ignition of coal, petroleum, and gas. Electrical energy introduced during the 1890s opened the door for other ways to run machinery.

A HISTORY OF THE BREWING INDUSTRY

Fermentation is an ancient form of biotechnology in which **microorganisms**—particularly certain types of microscopic fungi called yeasts—are used to convert one substance into a more desirable substance. Alcoholic beverages and provisions made by fermentation date back to prehistoric times. Every culture had a recipe for a condiment, drink, or food processed by microorganisms. One of the oldest is wine, which is made by adding yeast to the juice obtained from grapes and allowing the mixture to stand for a period of time. Wine jugs dating back to 5400 B.C. have been discovered in Iran. Large volumes of rice wine were produced in China around 2100 B.C. Starting in 800 B.C., vineyards and wineries appeared throughout Greece and France. Thus, the wine industry was born.

Public demand for wine prompted the development of technology for producing large amounts of wine with uniform quality and characteristics. The Phoenicians engaged in wine commerce throughout the Middle East. Similarly, the Chinese traded rice wine throughout Asia and possibly Europe. As the wine trade grew and spread, so too did the development, production, and trade of another alcoholic beverage: beer. It was not until A.D. 1516, however, that the brewing industry became fully realized. In 1516, German laws required all beers to be made from hops, malt, water, and a certain type of yeast. These laws were mainly passed to ensure a uniform and unique taste for German beers. Before these laws, beers tasted drastically different depending on the plants used for flavoring and the byproducts produced by the various yeast. Other cultures around the world began fermenting other alcoholic beverages for trade. Rum, a beverage made through the fermentation of sugarcane, became a huge industry.

Brewing became a modern industry in 1880 when French scientist Louis Pasteur discovered the chemistry behind fermentation. He developed a process called **sterilization** that killed disease-causing organisms in fermented products. Sterilization not only improved the quality of the beverages, but also allowed them to be stored for long periods without spoiling. It became possible to make larger quantities of beer that could be stored or shipped longer distances (Figure 5.1). The variety and quality of alcoholic beverages increased throughout the middle 1900s, as scientists developed a better understanding of biochemistry and new instruments were invented for analyzing chemicals. Wine makers were then able to determine how the chemicals found in wine influence taste.

Biotechnology entered the fermentation industry slowly because of public concerns about foods prepared with GMOs. Ultimately, however, two factors pushed biotechnology in commercial fermentation. One was the outbreak of illnesses and poisonings among people drinking alcoholic beverages caused by unexpected waste products formed by the yeast during the production process. The second was a growing desire for higher-quality products in a highly competitive market starting around the 1970s. New yeasts are being genetically modified to ensure the production of beverages that are safe and have consistent characteristics. This is done by adding or subtracting genes involved in the production of metabolic wastes. These GM yeasts are less likely to make toxic products such as glycol which can cause liver damage. Today, fermentation of industrial chemicals, but not beer, is almost wholly carried out by genetically modified yeasts.

Figure 5.1 Brewing became a modern industry in 1880 when Louis Pasteur discovered the chemistry of fermentation. It then became possible to make large volumes of beverages that did not spoil during storage and shipping. The large brewing tanks shown here are specially controlled environments where yeast produces beer by fermentation.

A HISTORY OF CLOTHING

Clothing was fundamental to survival as people headed toward new lands in colder, drier, and wetter climates. Archaeologists have discovered primitive tools called "spindles" in ancient ruins throughout the world. Spindles were used to make tight fibers from fur and plants. This finding indicates that people progressed to weaving clothing instead of wearing outfits made of animal skins and leaves. Better fibers were obtained by selectively breeding plants and animals to produce better raw materials to make textile fibers (material used to make fabric for carpeting, clothing, and other purposes). The invention of the spinning wheel around A.D. 500 in India gave rise to the textile industry. Textiles immediately gained favor in international trade, becoming a major item exchanged between Africa, Asia, and Europe. The Industrial Revolution led to the invention of looms and high-speed weaving machinery. During this period, synthetic dyes, which allowed colors to be uniform, were invented and grew into a separate field of chemistry. Synthetic fibers such as neoprene and nylon came about during the mid-1950s.

In spite of the improving technology, textile manufacturers still had three major needs: comfortable fibers, colors that were safe and did not bleed or fade, and materials adapted for different types of weather conditions. In the 1980s, biotechnology provided solutions to these three concerns. First, new natural fibers were developed from GM aspen trees and cotton. Also, new synthetic fibers were developed, replacing the need for the fossil fuels as the raw materials used to make the older materials. Petroleum formed the chemical backbone of synthetic fibers. Biotechnology also led to the development of precolored fibers and dyes that resisted fading. Comfort and color were also improved by **bioprocessing** the fabrics with enzymes that soften the material and adjust the color. Currently, transgenic organisms are used in the production of lightweight silk fibers similar to Kevlar® that insulate from cold, protect from heat, reduce ultraviolet light and radiation exposure, and protect from trauma such as bullets, knives, and explosions.

THE COMPUTER AGE

In the 1980s, high powered computers made it possible for biotechnology to progress to its current stage. **Supercomputers** handle the large volumes of data needed in biotechnology research. **Bioinformatics** is the use of computers to manage biological information and is invaluable to biological research, particularly genetic research. Computers also drive much of the laboratory equipment and machinery needed to run biotechnology operations. Just as computers helped advance biotechnology, so too has biotechnology contributed to improvements in computer technology. Certainly the potential for computers to manage the large amounts of information being generated by biotechnology labs generated incentives for improvements in computer processing. The first computers started out not as machines but as mathematical shortcuts used in engineering buildings and devices. An instrument called a "slide rule" was a hand-operated tool invented in 1620 that permitted rapid complex calculations. The abacus, another ancient calculator, also allowed for complex calculations (Figure 5.2). Then, Blaise Pascal invented a crude form of the adding machine in 1642. Pendulum clocks for keeping accurate time followed these inventions. Pascal was a French mathematician who invented many things including the barometer for measuring atmospheric pressure. Electronic computers did not get their start until the dawn of electricity in the 1880s. The first machine used was a manually operated computational machine used for tabulating census data.

The early 1900s saw the development of a host of electrical circuit devices, including diodes, transmitters, triodes, and television tubes. This paved the way for the first true electrical computing device, developed by German engineer Konrad Zuse in 1938. **Transistors**, which were used to make faster and smaller computers, were invented in 1947. Circuitry leading to personal computers and pocket calculators emerged in 1971. Better circuit designs permitted engineers to develop the computers commonly used today. Scientists today have pushed electrical circuitry to new size limits. The 1990s saw the emergence of a new science called **nanotechnology**, which involves designing miniature computers and machines. The term *nano* refers to a very small unit of metric measure. The use of biotechnology principles and methods in nanotechnology has led to another new science, **bionanotechnology.**

Figure 5.2 Modern methods of performing mathematical calculations are very different from the ancient methods, such as using an abacus (shown here). Nanobiotechnology is a field dedicated to developing new ways of designing miniature computers and machines. Ultimately, the traditional electrical circuit computer may be replaced by one run by biochemicals and cell components.

This field uses biological molecules and the components of cells as miniature computers and machines that drive microscopic robots having possible medical value.

> ### Stop and Consider
>
> Try to imagine life if all energy was still provided by animals, humans, and water. How would the following aspects of your daily life change?
> - Mailing a letter off to a friend.
> - Going to a restaurant to get a quick meal.
> - Sitting at home at night to read a book.
> - Visiting a relative 500 miles away.

Early attempts at bionanotechnology in the beginning of the 1990s used antibodies to determine the presence of other molecules. Eventually by the end of the 1990s, scientists used whole cells and parts of cells to determine the chemistry of solutions. Now scientists are using carbohydrates, lipids, proteins, and nucleic acids to build tiny robotic machines called **nanomachines**. It is believed that nanomachines can be placed in other machinery or inside of organisms to monitor and repair damage due to wear and tear or injury. DNA is currently being used in devices called **microarrays** that can detect particular chemicals or even the DNA sequence of an organism. Special enzymes that work like small tools are the components that can be used as artificial body tissues such as synthetic muscle fibers. Circuits built from biochemicals are proving to be as reliable as traditional circuits; biological circuits, however, can be made much smaller and faster.

FOOD PRESERVATION

The inability to store food adequately was one of the biggest barriers to large-scale food production and commerce. In early times, food had to be eaten where it was produced. Spoilage claimed any food that was stored or shipped for too long. Food preservation involved drying, fermenting, or salting. Unfortunately, these techniques changed the taste of the food, making some food unpalatable. Sometimes food was cooked in an attempt to slow down spoilage. Early in human history food, preservation was needed to conduct the food trade and commerce taking place in the 1500s. There were mounting incentives to develop better food preservation methods. In the early 1800s, a Boston entrepreneur named Frederic Tudor proposed using ice to preserve food shipped to warmer climates. Since there was no refrigeration at that time, the ice was collected in the winter from rural New England. By the mid-1800s, the Industrial Revolution had introduced bottling, canning, and refrigeration.

Traditional chemistry made the first modern contributions to long-term food preservation. Dozens of chemical food preservatives appeared around the 1940s. Food preservatives worked by either reducing the chemistry of natural spoilage or by restricting the growth of microorganisms that decay food. Natural spoilage is due to the breakdown of food molecules interacting with oxygen in the air. Unfortunately, many of these chemicals alter the taste of the food or may be harmful to the health if consumed in large amounts. Biotechnology came about with some solutions to these problems. First, crops that spoiled more slowly were developed. This involved altering ripening genes or genetically manipulating the chemistry of the plants to slow down decay by microorganisms. Today, fruits and vegetables are being genetically modified to produce chemicals called **antioxidants**. Antioxidants are edible chemicals that slow down the natural decay of substances. Some plants are being bred to fight off disease. Many plant diseases contribute to rapid rotting. Meat preservation lagged behind crop developments because of the difficulty in reducing the breakdown of animal muscle tissue. Special bacterial secretions that bind certain metals and salts are being investigated for preserving meats. Also, certain drugs produced using biotechnology and given to animals before slaughter are proving to reduce meat spoilage. One drug interacts with the nervous system of pigs causing them to be less stressed before being slaughtered. Stress causes pigs to produce chemicals that alter the flavor of the pork products.

A HISTORY OF MATERIALS

Materials include a diverse array of substances that can be used for manufacturing appliances, buildings, machines, textiles, tools, and utensils. Raw rock, soil, and wood were the first materials used by people. These substances were used to produce housing, pottery, and simple tools. In 3000 B.C., people learned to purify metals and the minerals collected from rock. These refined materials proved useful in constructing the first tools for hunting and food preparation. One ancient material, asphalt, was found in volcanic regions and used as an adhesive. It eventually became a paving material for roads. Copper was the first material to be used for manufacturing tools, followed by bronze in 2000 B.C. Pewter and steel were developed in 1000 B.C. Pewter is a mixture of lead and tin while steel is iron combined with other elements. Each civilization made use of metals independently. Materials became an industry and a popular unit of commerce with the birth of **metallurgy**—the science of obtaining and preparing metal for practical use. People with metallurgical skills manufactured metal objects for barter and money. New ovens designed for making metals also led to the development of glass (made from heated sand and other minerals) in Greece and porcelain (made from heated clay and ceramics) in China.

Metals and minerals were the predominant materials until modern chemistry came about in the mid-1800s, when people learned to make the first synthetic materials using special chemical reactions. These new materials were primarily used in textiles. Vulcanized rubber (invented in 1839) and plastic (invented in 1909) created a materials revolution. New synthetic materials continued to be developed throughout the 20th century.

Biotechnology methods have been applied to the materials sciences. Scientists are developing microorganisms that secrete synthetic chemicals to replace traditional textiles and plastic materials. Biotechnology can create these molecules without using petroleum products as a starting material. Microorganisms require less energy and produce fewer pollutants than do synthetic chemistry processes. For instance a plastic-like material called polylactate results in many potentially dangerous wastes when made synthetically. Microorganisms produce the same chemical without producing toxic wastes. Biotechnology is also helping the production of traditional materials (Figure 5.3). Scientists use microorganisms to collect metals and minerals more effectively from mines without destroying the land with toxic chemicals. They can now use microorganisms that break down the rock separating the minerals. Genetically modified trees are producing better quality fibers for use in paper and wood products.

A HISTORY OF FOSSIL FUELS

Growing civilizations battled with the potential for wood shortages immediately upon discovering its use as an energy source. This started to become a problem for urban areas that needed the wood as both a material and as fuel for running machinery. The invention of steam engines and the ensuing railroad boom further stressed wood supplies throughout the world. This drove people to burn coal as an energy source to power the machinery of the Industrial Revolution. Coal, however, proved to be dirty and was ineffective in certain machines. Scientists started looking for other sources of fuel. Petroleum was not an effective energy source until the early 1800s. New machines had to be developed to use the oil, plus chemists had to peform chemical treatements on the oil to make it a more versatile fuel. The crude oil collected from the ground was

Figure 5.3 Rubber was originally a natural product tapped from rubber trees, such as those shown here growing in an Asian plantation. Modern chemistry came up with ways to produce synthetic rubber. However, the process of making synthetic rubber uses a lot of petroleum and produces many pollutants.

almost useless in machines, as it contained impurities that would interfere with the machine's function.

The great demand for oil created periodic shortages and increased its cost significantly. Once again, people looked for other energy sources. The ancient methods of harnessing water and wind energy became valuable again, but they were restricted to providing energy for individual homes or small communities. Solar energy emerged as a new source of energy, but it too had limitations. Newer energy sources include nuclear energy and hydrogen cell technology.

One obstacle to the use of a new energy source, however, is that the powerplants have to be redesigned to utilize these energy sources. Also, there are dangers associated with some alternative energy sources—perhaps most notably, radioactive materials and tanks of hydrogen gas. At first, biotechnology played accessory roles in the oil industry. For example, genetically modified organisms were used to clean up oil spills, and DNA molecules were added to oil as a signature to identify particular oil supplies (this helped give proof of ownership if oil was spilled or stolen). Today, biotechnology researchers are looking at using microorganisms to provide power. One strategy involves having **microorganisms** or plants produce oils with the same properties as the oil collected by wells. Some researchers are collecting electricity produced by feeding yeast. Under certain growing conditions yeast will generate electricity from the sugars they normally use to provide themselves with energy. This process is very similar to fermentation. The U.S. Department of Energy recently provided funding for scientists to tap into solar energy by creating artificial plants. Traditional solar cells are expensive and contain hazardous chemicals. The artificial plants' solar panels can be grown with little cost and do not use dangerous materials.

Stop and Consider

Job skills change as societies adopt new technologies for running their civilizations. How do you think biotechnology will affect the job skills of tomorrow?

A HISTORY OF MEDICAL TECHNOLOGY

The ability to diagnose illness is fundamental to modern medicine. Modern medicine would not have been possible without the belief that illness had natural causes, a concept that originated with the Greek physician Hippocrates in 420 B.C. Unfortunately, this idea was replaced by previously held beliefs that illnesses were punishment for sins. Little was done with disease diagnosis until people started dissecting animals and humans from A.D. 180 through the 1600s. As people began to understand how the body worked, disease diagnosis and even cures started to emerge. Also, the discovery of microorganisms throughout the 1700s and 1800s contributed to the treatment of infectious diseases. People learned that infectious diseases can be controlled by killing or preventing contact with the organism. Medical diagnosis up until the 1890s mostly involved simple examinations that used very little technology. Prior to the development of a chemistry based pharmaceutical industry in the early 20th century, treatments were limited to herbs and toxic substances. People learned to prevent disease with vaccination starting in 1796. In the mid-1800s, chemists working with physicians helped develop specific medications to treat illness. The first use of antibiotics in 1941 marked the introduction of biotechnology in medicine. These chemicals derived from fungi were not fully used until the 1940s.

Biotechnology first made its way into medical technology through its use in disease diagnosis. Traditional diagnosis used special chemical analyses and microbial detection equipment. Enzymes attached to special membranes were used to rapidly detect certain diseases and microbes. They proved accurate, effective, and inexpensive. The test kits were also portable and could even by used by patients (for eample, glucose home monitoring test stips for diabetes). The home pregnancy test is an extension of a technology called **enzyme linked immunosorbant assay** (ELISA, Figure 5.4). Biotechnology is now being integrated into traditional medical diagnostic machinery to improve its speed and accuracy. New types of drugs and vaccines are being made inexpensively using biotechnology procedures. A growing body of evidence shows that the drugs made using biotechnological methods are safer than those made with traditional methods. They have fewer impurities than

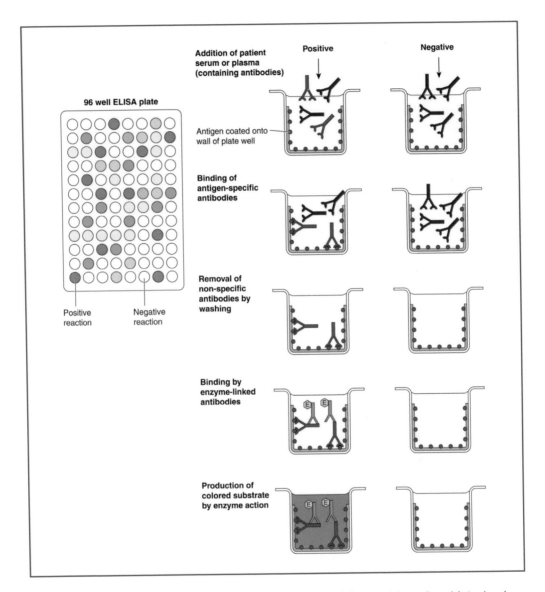

Figure 5.4 ELISA (enzyme linked immunosorbant assay) is a test based on biotechnology principles. Samples tested with ELISA turn color if they contain a specific antibody. The home pregnancy test is an older application of this form of biotechnology. Similar devices are being used for a variety of purposes including the detection of genetic diseases and environmental pollutants.

those made using synthetic chemistry. Plus, drugs made in cell cultures are less likely to pass along diseases found in animals used for traditional drug production. Bionanotechnology is currently working its way into medical diagnosis and treatment. Miniature biological robots are being developed to detect illness and carry out therapeutic (healing) tasks from within the body.

CONNECTIONS

Biotechnology produced a rebirth of commercial and industrial technologies. It showed how the metabolism of various organisms could fabricate some of the same chemicals made using chemical processes and manufacturing machinery. Today, biotechnology is used in the manufacturing of beverages, commercial chemicals, dyes, foods, medicines, and textiles. Advances in biotechnology are leading to devices that may even replace computers.

FOR MORE INFORMATION

For more information about the concepts discussed in this chapter, search the Web using the following keywords:

Biobusiness, Bioprocessing, Bioinformatics, Nanotechnology, Bionanotechnolgy

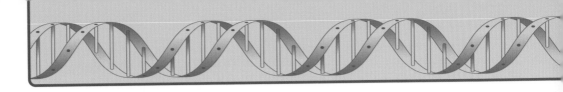

6

Industrial Applications of Biotechnology

Throughout history, consumer needs and demands have driven manufacturing activities. Early in human history, the needs were generally associated with survival. As civilization flourished, however, industry started focusing on products that made life easier, more comfortable, or more enjoyable. In this regard, industrial biotechnology is no different. It was born out of the desire to efficiently create products that directly or indirectly satisfy the needs and wants of people. **Direct products** go immediately to the consumer. **Indirect products** serve other industries that produce direct consumer goods. Direct products fall into many categories of everyday items that many people take for granted: automobiles, books, CDs, food, gasoline, radios, and toys are all examples of direct consumer commodities. Indirect goods are not as obvious or visible. Building materials, clothing fibers, dyes, oils, paints, and electrical wiring are indirect products that help manufacturers make other products of value to consumers. Industrial biotechnology is playing an increasingly important role in the manufacturing of these items.

Industrial biotechnology, which is also called **bioprocessing**, differs from other types of manufacturing because it uses cells, components of cells, or microorganisms to create products. The theory of consumer bioprocessing dates back 8,000 years, when the first beer was brewed in vats. Ancient people recognized that it took certain conditions to convert the components of mashed up plant wastes into alcohol. It was discovered by Louis Pasteur in the 1850s that the conditions favored fermentation by microorganisms. Modern bioprocessing, however, did not get its start until the early 1900s with the birth of biochemistry. Louis Pasteur and other scientists identified the specific components of cell metabolism that were responsible for bioprocessing activities (Figure 6.1). Thus, whole living cells were not needed anymore. Later it was learned that enzymes carried out each stage of metabolism. Bioprocessing using gene technology is still in its infancy. It applies the genetic engineering knowledge gained in the 1980s to the development of organisms capable of producing a variety of chemicals. These novel organisms are engineered to perform the desired metabolic processes.

In many countries, industrial biotechnology is categorized into specific manufacturing categories called **platforms**. Platforms are carried out by whole organisms, cells, or components of cells; their focus is to make the specific biotechnology product needed by that particular industry. One of the oldest platforms is the Yeast Industry Platform (YIP), which combines genetically modified yeast with traditional methods to make products from whole yeast cells grown in culture. Related to the YIP is the Fungal Industry Platform (FIP), which uses fungi other than yeast to carry out a multitude of functions. Fungi were used in ancient times to produce cheese flavorings and to process soy sauce and other foods. Three other microbial

Figure 6.1 The findings of Louis Pasteur (shown here in his lab) and other scientists around the early 1900s showed that specific fractions of cell metabolism were responsible for bioprocessing activities. Before that time, scientists thought that whole living cells were needed to carry out metabolic processes.

platforms are the Bacillus subtilis Genome Platform (BACIP), the Lactic Acid Bacteria Industry Platform (LABIP), and the Industry Platform for Microbiology (IPM). BSCIP and LABIP use specific bacteria that are easily grown in large vats. They are metabolically engineered to produce a variety of chemicals and to remove waste products from other industrial operations. LABIP is being investigated for the production of biodegradable and recyclable plastics.

Agricultural biotechnology gave rise to the Farm Animal Industry Platform (FAIP) and the Plant Industry Platform (PIP). Both platforms use genetically modified animals and plants to produce commercial chemicals, drugs, fibers, and food. Related to these platforms is the Animal Cell Industry Platform (ACIP), which uses cultured animal cells to produce products. PIP currently covers plant cells grown in culture. Ultimately, a separate division called the Plant Cell Industry Platform may develop as this technology matures. A special platform called the *In Vitro* Testing Industry Platform (IVTIP) uses animal, microbial, and plant cells for medical testing. One function of this platform is the investigation of techniques for performing chemical safety and medical testing on cells instead of in animals and humans. The Environmental Biotechnology Industry Platform (EBIP) also uses a variety of organisms and components of organisms. Instead of producing a product, however, EBIP uses bioprocessing technology to clean the environment and reduce pollution. Environmental bioprocessing is also called **bioremediation**. The platform terminology is not used regularly in the United States even though the same types of biotechnologies are being developed.

BIOPROCESSING OPERATIONS

Companies that perform bioprocessing do not at first glance look much different from traditional commercial operations. In most cases, they use similar equipment and perform many of the same techniques. One important difference is the care bioprocessing companies must take to maintain the cells, cell components, and organisms used in industrial biotechnology. Special considerations must be given to keep the bioprocessing systems free of any contaminating microorganisms that can spoil the operations. In addition, it is important to ensure that the processes used do not create problems for humans or the environment. Whereas years of experience and research have provided much information about the pollution produced by traditional industrial operations, there is much yet to learn about the effects of industrial biotechnology on the environment. Each country has strict guidelines for carrying out industrial biotechnology operations.

Stop and Consider

Do you think it is possible to produce large cultures of human cells for bioprocessing? What would be the purpose of using human cells this way for biotechnology?

Traditional manufacturing requires machinery or synthetic chemical reactions to make a product. Synthetic chemical reactions involve specific chemical reactions that were developed to produce a particular product. For example, the drug acetaminophen (Tylenol®) used to relieve headaches is made from chemicals called phenols found in coal tar. Coal tar is a thick, black liquid obtained after coal is heated to high temperatures in a liquid. Biotechnology manufacturing differs from traditional manufacturing in that it uses biochemical reactions, cells, or whole organisms to make the products. Machinery and some synthetic chemical reactions are needed in biotechnology to either assist the process or purify the final product. For instance, the biotechnology products may be pumped into **centrifuges** or **filters** that separate the product from unwanted substances. Bioprocessing can be used to make large quantities of chemicals that at one time could only be extracted in small amounts from organisms or synthesized using complex or expensive chemical processes.

Each bioprocessing operation is performed using a series of very specific steps. The steps for a particular type of bioprocessing vary depending on the product being made or the location of the waste being cleaned. One type of bioprocessing called "**extraction**" involves removing the desired chemicals from an organism. It is used in the the food supplement and pharmaceutical industries to produce vitamins and drugs. One example is the collection and processing of insulin (used in the treatment of diabetes) from the pancreas of sheep.

Insulin secreted by bacteria can now be produced in large vats. The traditional method involved extracting insulin from the pancreas of pigs or sheep. Unfortunately, insulin is found in very small amounts in pancreas. To avoid these problems, a company could make insulin using synthetic chemicals (Figure 6.2). This process, however, is very expensive and must be controlled carefully to ensure that adequate amounts of insulin are produced. It also usually produces wastes that pose a pollution risk to the air and water. In spite of these drawbacks, synthetic chemical processing is favored over extraction because there is no chance of passing along undetected chemicals or diseases. An additional problem with synthetic chemical processing is that it produces some biochemical end products that are shaped differently than the desired product. This is significant because the differently shaped products— which are called **chiral isomers**—do not work the same way in the human body as does the normal molecule. Chiral isomers are ineffective, and in come cases can cause illness. The chiral isomers can be separated using a technique called **chiral chromatography.**

Bioprocessing of insulin using genetically modified organisms applies the best aspects of the extraction and synthesis methods. This combined method produces a purer product than can be achieved with either of the individual processes. A significant benefit of this

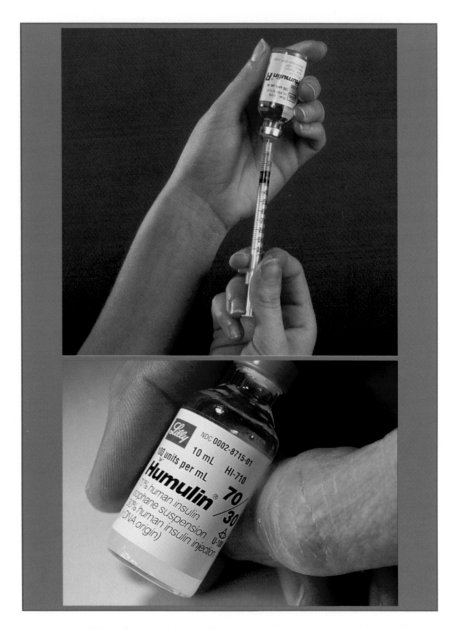

Figure 6.2 Diabetics would not live long without regular injections of insulin. Most insulin today is made using genetic engineering. Humulin® is produced using microorganisms containing a human gene for insulin.

method is that scientists are able to genetically engineer cells that can produce unique products. Eventually, it may be possible to use this combined process to produce many chemicals that are currently made through synthetic chemical processing. Unfortunately, the research needed to develop this technique is very expensive and requires a specialized knowledge of genetic engineering and cell culture. Not all companies or nations have the resources to pursue such biotechnology.

ENVIRONMENTAL BIOTECHNOLOGY

Environmental bioprocessing is not carried out to produce material. It uses organisms to clean up environmental wastes. The wastes can be cleaned either before they enter the environment or after they enter the environment and become a pollutant. Genetically modified plants were recently developed that break down explosives in their roots.

Environmental bioprocessing operations differ depending on the type and location of the waste. Off-site or *in vitro* environmental processing cleans wastes using industrial machinery similar to that used in product manufacturing. The polluted soil or water is removed from the area and cleaned at a facility. *In situ* environmental bioprocessing is used to clean up air, soil, and water pollution. *In situ* means "taking place in the original location," so **in situ bioprocessing** refers to cleanup that is performed directly in the environment. In off-site, or *in vitro* environmental bioprocessing, the waste that needs to be broken down is identified through chemical analysis. It may take years for pollutants to break down without intervention. Bioremediation can break down the pollutant in days to several weeks. A biochemical or microorganism capable of safely breaking down the waste, called a **bioremediation agent**, is identified from databases posted by governmental organizations and universities and tested to confirm its effectiveness against the targeted waste chemical. This database is also useful for exploring possible organisms that may break down chemicals not currently being treated with bioremediation. The University of Minnesota has a bioremediation organism database located at http://umbbd.ahc.umn.edu/aboutBBD.html. The bioremediation agent is also tested to make sure that it does not break the waste chemical down into components that are just as toxic as the original waste. Once the tests confirm the bioremediation agent's suitability, microorganisms capable of producing the bioremediation agent—usually bacteria or fungi—are identified. These microorganisms are modified through selective breeding or genetic engineering to create a population capable of rapidly breaking down the waste. These organisms are sometimes called **superbugs**. There are companies that produce and sell these organisms for specific wastes. A pilot study is conducted to determine whether the bioengineered microorganism (or the bioremediation agent extracted from it) is able to break down the waste. If the pilot study is successful, the cleanup operation is undertaken. Cleanup can be performed in various ways:

- Collect polluted soil or water and add it to a large tank containing the organism or the extracted bioremediation agent.

- Add the organism or the extracted bioremediation agent to a machine, motor, tank, or vessel containing the waste.

- Place agricultural or industrial waste in a holding tank containing the organism or the extracted bioremediation agent.

The procedure for *in situ* environmental bioprocessing is similar to that for off-site environmental processing. Some differences are the potential use of plants in addition to bacteria or fungi as bioremediation agents, a process called phytoremediation. In some cases, genes from bacteria and fungi are added to plants to improve their phytoremediation capabilities. Another difference is that pilot studies are conducted not only to assess the ability of the organism or bioremediation agent to break down the waste under laboratory conditions, but also to determine their effectiveness in breaking

That Is One "Hot" Enzyme!

A host of unique creatures are being discovered as more and more scientists conduct deep-sea explorations of underwater volcanoes in the Pacific Ocean. Scientists were surprised at the amount of life found in such severe and unforgiving environmental conditions. How severe and unforgiving are the conditions around these volcanoes (called deep-sea vents)? The vents reach temperatures hot enough to easily melt plastic and blister human skin. The water pressure around the vents can crush flat the sturdiest submarine. And the water is so acidic from the high amounts of sulfur that it can irritate flesh. These are not favorable conditions for most organisms. Scientists are very interested in studying the specialized biochemicals that help deep-sea vent organisms adapt to this extreme environment. Scientists believe there may be industrial applications for these unique biochemicals.

Certain industrial applications use machines that operate under extreme conditions. These machines sometimes become dirty and require frequent cleaning. This usually means stopping the machine and taking it apart, which takes it out of operation at a cost of productivity and profit to the company. Also, the parts are usually cleaned with hazardous chemicals that must be carefully used and disposed of in a way that does not harm the environment. Many of the chemicals that clog machinery are organic molecules capable of being degraded with enzymes. Enzymes are safe and biodegradable. They break down organic molecules into smaller chemicals that do not pollute the environment. This biotechnology application saves companies money, and has even made its way into laundry detergents used in the home. But, like other chemicals, enzymes still require companies to stop the machinery before they can be used. It would be beneficial to have a way of cleaning the machines while they are still operating. This is where biotechnology offers another solution. Enzymes from deep-sea vent organisms can operate under the extreme conditions created by the machines as they are operating. Consequently, scientists have used these enzymes to develop cleaning agents that can be placed in industrial machinery while it is running. These enzymes may ultimately find their way into automotive oils and other machines used in everyday life.

down the waste where the waste is located in the environment. Tests are also conducted to ensure that the organisms do not cause harm to the environment. Cleanup is performed by growing the organisms at the waste site or by adding the bioremediation agent to the waste. After the cleanup operation is performed, regular testing is conducted to ensure that the waste is being broken down and is safe to dispose.

Stop and Consider

Think about how you could use the following technologies around your house for everyday purposes:
- **Traditional bioprocessing**
- **Synthetic bioprocessing**
- *In situ* **environmental bioprocessing**

Bioremediation is used extensively today. It regularly makes the news when it is applied to agricultural chemical spills, highway accidents, oil tanker spills, radioactive waste contamination, and train wrecks (Figure 6.3). In some cases, it is possible to encourage the growth of natural bioremediation organisms in the areas where wastes are found.

CONNECTIONS

Bioprocessing refers to industrial manufacturing procedures that rely on biotechnology. It differs from traditional manufacturing because it uses cells, components of cells, or microorganisms to create the products. Fermented foods were the first bioprocessed materials, dating back 8,000 years. Modern bioprocessing has progressed greatly from the crude procedures carried out in the past. Ancient bioprocessing was carried out in cooking vessels. Today, bioprocessing is conducted in sterile vats using cells or microbes grown under precise conditions.

Figure 6.3 *In situ* (on-site) environmental bioprocessing or bioremediation was instrumental in cleaning up large oil spills in Alaska, Florida, Louisiana, and Texas. Italy, Russia, and Spain have also used it on spills along beaches and lakes. This technique was important for reducing the amount of wildlife killed by the oil.

The bioprocessing industry is divided into various manufacturing processes. An internationally used term called "platform" is used to describe the process. Each platform produces a particular product and is supported by research unique to the processes used in the platform. Some governments have separate regulations controlling the quality and safety of each platform.

FOR MORE INFORMATION

For more information about the concepts discussed in this chapter, search the Web using the following keywords:

Consumer biotechnology, Commercial biotechnology, Humulin, *In situ* bioprocessing, Phytoremediation

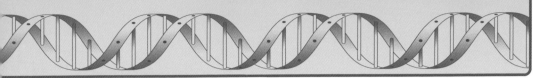

7

Biotechnology and Consumer Products

Today, it is very difficult to live in any country without being affected by some aspect of biotechnology. Biotechnology is one of the fastest growing industries, matched only by the computer sector. It is also one of the youngest sciences and has relied on the mingling of agriculture, biochemistry, biology, chemistry, computer science, economics, genetics, and physics. Commercial applications of biotechnology had been foreseen in the early 1970s, long before fundamental biotechnology principles were understood or biotechnology technologies perfected. By the early 1980s, biotechnology developments were working their way directly into consumer products. At first, biotechnology methods were used to produce drugs such as **erythropoietin** for treating **anemia** and insulin for treating diabetes. Anemia is a condition in which people are not producing adequate amounts of red blood cells needed to carry oxygen. Only a few people needed these drugs, so biotechnology went largely undetected by most of society. It was so unknown that allied health workers, pharmacists, and physicians had to be educated about the new biotechnology drugs.

Biotechnology was thrust into the public eye in the mid-1980s when special interest groups protested the first biotechnology applications used on crops. Scientists in the United States gained infamy for testing a genetically modified (GM) bacterium on crops intended for human consumption. One bacterium was GM to act as antifreeze on strawberry crops. It was designed to inhibit the growth of other bacteria that caused ice crystals to form on the leaves of certain crops. A secretion produced by the natural bacteria encouraged cold water on the leaves to form ice. The ice crystals damaged the leaves, making the plants susceptible to fungal and viral diseases. This drastically reduced strawberry yield. The "Ice Minus" bacteria lacked the ice-promoting secretion, thereby reducing the incidence of ice crystal formation. Pictures of the scientists applying the ICE Minus bacteria to a test field and the EPA scientists supervising the test, all wearing safety space suits were widely published, raising both unintended and unnecessary alarm.

People decried these biotechnology applications for two reasons: one was concern about the potential environmental damage caused by the novel bacteria. The other was fear that the bacteria could cause disease in animals and humans.

Several years after Ice Minus caught public attention, biotechnology made another attempt at marketing consumer products. This time, a genetically altered tomato called the Flavr Savr developed by Monsanto was introduced into the United Kingdom by Zeneca Corporation. The tomato contained a GM gene that slowed ripening without reducing flavor. Other biotechnology crops and animals were in planning when the Flavr Savr was being sold. Again, the public did not warmly receive the new technology. In fact, the technology sparked fierce protests and litigation to limit the sale of the biotechnology foods. The foods were given the ignoble name "Frankenfoods" by protesters and the media.

Frankenfoods is the name coined by protesters for any genetically modified food (Figure 7.1).

Although biotechnology in the consumer products sector did not get a warm welcome, its applications in medicine and the non-food item sector were greeted with enthusiasm. By 1990, the U.S. government even permitted the first genetic engineering on a human in an attempt to treat a disease called **adenosine deaminase deficiency** which had left a young girl named Ashanti de Silva without an immune system. She would have died very young from common diseases without any treatment. The normal gene was placed in her blood cells giving her the ability to fight disease. This disease is normally treated with regular injections of a drug called pegylated bovine ADA.

Biotechnology companies learned the hard way that marketing directly to consumers is not as easy as selling a new washing machine or car. People today are very concerned about the effects of technology on their health and well-being. They are also skeptical about "new and improved" technologies using science that is difficult to understand. The history of consumer marketing is rife with examples of products that failed or that took a long time to earn public trust and acceptance. Even the ubiquitous automobile was greatly distrusted when it was first invented. It was thought to be less reliable than horses and trains, and the technology seemed too complicated to be feasible. Home computers would not be present in almost every household today if their developers accepted public skepticism about the idea of a reliable personal computer. As with biotechnology, the first personal computers were commercial flops. It took a many modifications and persistent marketing to make computers a common commodity.

HOW BIOTECHNOLOGY FITS INTO
THE CONSUMER PRODUCTS INDUSTRY

Economists and government agencies define the consumer products industry as any company that designs, manufactures, or

Figure 7.1 The public did not warmly receive the genetically altered Flavr Savr tomato. Violent protests and litigation resulted from the sale of this biotechnology food. Foods such as the Flavr Savr tomato were dubbed "Frankenfoods" by their detractors.

markets any of several common household items, including but hardly limited to apparel, cleaning products, appliances, electronics, furniture, hand and power tools, housewares, instruments, personal care products, pet products, sporting goods, and toys. Other economic sectors include agriculture, commercial products, energy, health care, medicine, and transportation. Biotechnology is developing applications for every economic sector; however, the consumer products sector has the greatest growth potential for biotechnology. Consumer products have a high earning potential for companies that successfully market their commodities.

What inroads has biotechnology made in the consumer products industry? Many of the contributions of biotechnology go unnoticed and are mostly associated with improvements in traditional manufacturing processes. The following sectors of the consumer products industry are either benefiting already or expect to see improvements from advances in biotechnology:

- Apparel: Biotechnology has contributed to the development of new fibers used in making clothing. New types of cotton that do not need artificial dyes are being investigated. Clothing made from these fibers will not fade. Sheep that produce wool that is more comfortable are being developed, as are silkworms that make silk fiber that is more durable. A gene for spider silk protein has been placed in other cells for bioprocessing, with the aim of producing fibers that can be used to make tear-resistant clothing. Prefaded blue jeans get their color from treatment with biotechnology enzymes extracted from fungi found in nature.

- Automobile products: The first biotechnology automobile product was a windshield antifreeze solution composed of biodegradable bacterial secretions that prevent ice formation. It is not as toxic as the alcohols used in traditional antifreeze. The transportation industries have tested it on airlines, trains, and trucks. Some gasoline and motor oil additives are being manufactured by bacteria in **bioreactors**. Researchers are looking into plastics made of polylactic acid secreted by GM bacteria. These plastics are environmentally safer to manufacture and will make cars lighter in weight and therefore more fuel efficient.

set by their trade partners. Some guidelines restricted the use of genetically modified organisms (GMOs) in foods for human consumption. For example, GM corn could not be used in European countries directly to make human food, although it can be used in agricultural animal feed. Raw materials or ingredients made through genetic technology must be identified so they can be traced in any consumer product. Many countries label all consumer goods made using biotechnology. Especially important to consumers are labels on GM animals and plants used to make food (Figure 7.2). The European Union is currently more strict than the United States about labeling GM foods.

A majority of consumers worldwide buy biotechnology products without knowledge of the product's biotechnology origins. Various groups in different countries have conducted public surveys about biotechnology and biotechnology products. Overall the surveys showed that less than half of the people surveyed understood the technology used to make biotechnology products. More than half of the public is uncertain about using biotechnology products. Most were uncertain of the dangers because they claimed that they did not know enough to make a judgment. Others are fearful of unknown risks. A small percentage of the public avidly supports biotechnology whereas an equal percentage fully opposes it for ethical or religious reasons. Negative public sentiment is not stopping the advance of biotechnology into the consumer products manufacturing sector.

CONNECTIONS

Modern biotechnology is one of the fastest growing industries in the world. Many countries are vying for their share of the biotechnology market. Biotechnology is a young science that is quickly changing the way agriculture and industrial manufacturing is performed. Biotechnology was virtually unknown to the public until it made the news in the 1980s with the advent of the first genetically

Figure 7.2 Due to personal concerns about genetically modified foods, some people specifically look for foods with labels stating that they do not contain genetically modified ingredients.

modified microbes used to protect crops from frost damage. Next, genetically modified crops containing either altered genes or genes from other organisms emerged. All of these innovations met some public resistance because people feared the use of such technologies on consumer products. In contrast, biotechnology applications in

Labeling Genetically Modified Foods

Food labeling is a serious concern for food manufacturing companies. The U.S. Food and Drug Administration's (FDA) Nutrition Labeling and Education Act of 1990 requires that all foods have accurate reporting of a food's nutritional content. This means that a consumer must be able to tell how many carbohydrates, fats, fiber, proteins, sodium, and vitamins a food contains by reading its label. Food labeling regulations were enacted by the federal government in 1990 to give consumers the chance to make informed decisions about healthy eating. Now the federal government is being com-pelled by public interest groups to identify foods made from genetically modified organisms. These foods are unofficially called GM foods. Such a policy already exists in the European Union (EU). The EU believes that people have the right to make food safety choices. They see the labeling of GM foods as no different from the labeling of foods for religious dietary restrictions. Both the EU and the United States have food safety guidelines designed to let people know if a food contains ingredients that could cause allergies. Because of this policy, all foods containing egg and peanut products— common sources of food alergies—must be labeled accordingly. Biotechnology compa-nies, food producers, and most scientists oppose labels designed to identify foods that contain genetically modified organisms. To support this position, many people cite that there is no evidence indicating that GM foods cause allergies or any other health problems. Further, they note that GM food labels produce groundless fears in con-sumers. Studies in Europe showed that people thought the labels were there because the food was somehow dangerous. Currently, both sides disagree about the labeling of GM food. Some of the debate has been lessened by a new policy that redefines the desire to have the labeling. Now the governments are asking for the labels because they want people to have the information they may need to make ethical and moral choices about their diets. This is similar to the label information made available to vegetarians and people who follow religious dietary codes.

medicine and manufacturing of nonfood items were greeted with public enthusiasm. People began to realize the importance of biotechnology in prolonging life and decreasing the use of natural resources.

The consumer products market is going through a biotechnology revolution. Consumer products, such as apparel, appliances, eyeglasses, home furniture, tools, jewelry, linens, musical instruments, and toys, have some type of biotechnology component or their manufacturing was facilitated by biotechnology. Concerns about the safety of biotechnology led to the formation of recommendations concerning the sale of consumer biotechnology products. These recommendations were made by government agencies, public interest groups, and scientific organizations. Negative public sentiment about biotechnology is slowly declining because products have been proven to be effective and safe.

FOR MORE INFORMATION

For more information about the concepts discussed in this chapter, search the Web using the following keywords:

Ice Minus, Bt toxin, Flavr Savr Tomato, Consumer product safety

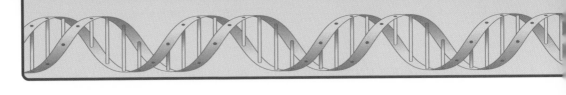

8

Controversial Issues in Biotechnology

Scientists have made great strides in agriculture, industry, medicine, and public health from the time when William Bateson coined the term *genetics* in 1905. Genetic research opened the door to the early biotechnology endeavors that took place in the early 1970s. Most of the scientific community welcomed the discoveries that emerged from the growing field of biotechnology. Many scientists adopted biotechnology into their research, greatly accelerating progress in many fields of biology and chemistry. Other scientists were more hesitant about biotechnology. They felt that the unknown risks outweighed biotechnology's benefits, however promising they might seem. A progression of meetings to discuss the ethics and safety of biotechnology began in 1974. The outcome of these meetings was the formulation of voluntary guidelines for conducting biotechnology properly and safely. Following this meeting, the United States National Institutes of Health (NIH) established DNA technology safety guidelines in 1976. All of these guidelines were designed to ensure that genetically modified organisms where handled in such a way as to not contaminate people or the environment.

Biotechnology innovations worked their way into society long before people were aware of the term "biotechnology" and the science behind its applications. In spite of this progression, these new developments attracted the attention of the news media. Biotechnology has been both praised and scrutinized in the news, generating considerable public debate. Scientists are generally not averse to controversy and deliberation. It is a regular part of formulating new hypotheses and testing new ideas. Unfounded bias for or against particular discoveries, on the other hand, can harm the advancement of science. Beliefs also influence the allocation of funding needed for further scientific progress. Stem cell researchers became all too aware of this phenomenon in 2003, when President George W. Bush banned research on new human fetal stem cell lines. President Bush did this because he objected to the use of human fetuses (a developing organism that is not capable of survival outside of the mother's body) in any type of research.

The controversial issues raised by biotechnology can be classified into three categories: safety, ethics, and morality (Figure 8.1). Safety issues are concerned with biotechnology's potential to adversely affect health and the environment. These issues are based on scientific information. Ethical issues address the positive and negative aspects of decisions and technological applications. Some people value the positive aspects (that is, the benefits) of agricultural biotechnology, believing that it is the best means of feeding people in developing nations. Other people focus on the various negative ethical impacts of biotechnology. For example, some people feel that it is unethical that developing nations could become economically dependent on technologies that they cannot afford to maintain. Moral issues are founded on religious beliefs. People who look at moral issues judge the "right or wrong" of

Figure 8.1 The public debate and political controversy raised by biotechnology can be classified into three categories: safety issues, ethical issues, and moral issues. Some people disagree with the use of biotechnology because of concerns raised by these issues.

societal decisions, using their religious beliefs as a benchmark. For many people, biotechnology has little to do with their moral convictions. Other people find that biotechnology goes against their religious teachings.

SAFETY ISSUES OF BIOTECHNOLOGY

A meeting called the Asilomar Conference held in 1975 showed the public that the scientific community was capable of evaluating the safety concerns of emerging technologies. This meeting was organized by scientists wishing to monitor genetic engineering research. The conference was named after the resort where it was held in Pacific Grove, California. At the time, California was the largest biotechnology research center in the world. Much of the genetic research that provided the foundation of biotechnology took place in the major universities around Los Angeles, San Diego, and San Francisco. Edwin Chargaff, one of the scientists who helped determine the genetic code, summarized the meeting saying, "This was probably the first time in history that the incendiaries formed their own fire brigade." He made this comment because scientists had traditionally conducted experiments without necessarily taking into account public concerns or sentiment. This public perception developed many years ago gave rise to the "mad scientist" image commonly portrayed in books, movies, and television shows such as Frankenstein. The Ansilomar meeting did not allay public skepticism about the safety of biotechnology.

One topic central to the Asilomar Conference was the safety of creating GM microorganisms. This was the only feasible biotechnology known at the time. Two fundamental research studies alerted the scientific community to this safety concern. The first was the production of recombinant DNA by Paul Berg and Herb Boyer in 1972. The second was an experiment conducted in 1974 by Annie Chang and Stanley Cohen, in which the first bacterium with recombinant DNA plasmids was created. Scientists immediately became alerted to the possible dangers of handling microorganisms with unknown characteristics. This was because nobody knew if these organisms had the potential to cause human disease or environmental harm. Although scientists today know more about the nature of recombinant microorganisms, this remains a concern. Today, the diversity of biotechnology techniques has broadened the safety concerns that must be addressed. Agricultural and industrial biotechnology applications share many safety concerns.

Biotechnology and Food Safety

Agricultural biotechnology safety issues are divided into public health concerns and environmental health concerns. Most countries around the world have governmental agencies and independent groups that address issues of food safety. The World Health Organization (WHO) of the United Nations (UN) works with these groups to conduct food safety programs worldwide. They are particularly concerned about food safety issues in developing nations that do not have adequate controls on food and drug production. There are five aspects of food safety:

1. Assurance of adequate food reserves to prevent shortages and famine.

2. Ensuring that food is safe to eat and will not cause any illness.

3. Ensuring that foods have adequate nutritional value and do not lead to malnutrition.

4. Protecting food supplies from intentional destruction and terrorist activities.

5. Investigating the environmental impacts of food production.

Recently, a surge in global terrorism has raised concerns food security. There is a fear that terrorists could target the nation's food supply by somehow poisoning or reducing the food supply. In response the United States Department of Agriculture Food Safety and Inspection Service set stiff penalties on anybody who knowingly tampers with food in a manner that can harm large segments of the population. These rules can be found at http://www.fsis.usda.gov/oa/topics/securityguide.htm. Some of these rules are used to prevent the intentional destruction of genetically modified plants by anti-GMO protestors.

In the United States, the Department of Agriculture (USDA) and the Food and Drug Administration (FDA) make food safety a primary mission. These agencies oversee the production of food and drugs manufactured in or imported to the Unites States, and have drafted thousands of pages of regulations to ensure that foods produced for animals and humans through biotechnology are safe. As mentioned earlier in Chapter 5 these regulations are compiled in the U.S. Codex of the Federal Register. These guidelines were enacted because of vocal public concerns about the safety of genetically altered foods. Researchers who develop GM organisms for agricultural use must provide documentation about the nutritional value and safety of the foods.

Stop and Consider

What are your feelings about eating genetically modified (GM) foods? If you have concerns, are they based on safety, ethical, or moral considerations?

These guidelines include measures that reduce the risk of allergic reactions, cancer, intolerances, microbial infection, and poisoning from food consumption. Some of these health risks are as much a product of the individual as is the food. For instance, at least 1% of the world's population has some type of **allergy** (Table 8.1). Allergies are caused by an overly sensitive immune system: The bodies of people with allergies treat certain chemicals as if they were a disease. As a result, the body mounts an inappropriately large immune response when it encounters the chemical. This immune response can cause a variety of illnesses, from a simple rash to life-threatening problems with breathing. All foods are tested to determine if they cause allergy. Biotechnology products are tested more stringently than other goods. Public misunderstanding of biotechnology has persuaded the government to test the allergic

Table 8.1 Common Food Allergies

Food allergy affects up to 6–8% of children under the age of three and 2% of adults. If you have an unpleasant reaction to something you have eaten, you might wonder if you have a food allergy. One out of three people either believe they have a food allergy or modify their or their family's diet. Thus, while food allergy is commonly suspected, healthcare providers diagnose it less frequently than most people believe.

In adults, the foods that most often cause allergic reactions include:

- Shellfish such as shrimp, crayfish, lobster, and crab
- Peanuts
- Tree nuts such as walnuts
- Fish
- Eggs

The most common foods that cause problems in children are:

- Eggs
- Milk
- Peanuts

Tree nuts and peanuts are the leading causes of deadly food allergy reactions called anaphylaxis.

Adults usually keep their allergies for life, but children sometimes outgrow them. Children are more likely to outgrow allergies to milk or soy, however, than allergies to peanuts or shrimp. The foods to which adults or children usually react are those foods they eat often. In Japan, for example, rice allergy is more frequent. In Scandinavia, codfish allergy is more common.

Source: U.S. Department of Health and Human Services, National Institutes of Health, National Institute of Allergy and Infectious Diseases

potential of GM foods even more extensively. So far, GM foods appear to have the same allergic potential as products manufactured through traditional means.

Government Regulation: Can Biotechnology Comply?

All manufacturers of consumer products must follow stringent government product safety guidelines. These guidelines protect consumers from being harmed by products. All of the guidelines are public information, available in a voluminous set of documents called the Codex of the Federal Register (CFR). For example, in the CFR there are guidelines stating that makeup must not cause skin damage. Other guidelines guard the environment from pollution produced during a product's manufacture and use. This same makeup must not harm animals in the wild after it is washed off the face and eventually exits the sewage treatment plant. The term *compliance* is used to describe manufacturing procedures that adhere to the government guidelines. It is not always easy coming up with comprehensive product safety guidelines. Usually, it takes months or years of testing to see if a product is completely safe. Most of the chemicals used in products manufactured through traditional methods are consistent in how they behave in safety testing. They are either safe or unsafe under certain types of conditions. Usually, the testing is uncomplicated and leads to few discrepancies in data. In contrast, biotechnology product manufacturing poses new problems for people developing safety guidelines. It is not easy testing the safety of biochemicals and genetically engineered organisms. The testing is very similar to the types done on pharmaceutical compounds. Biotechnology products are subject to more testing than are products produced through traditional means. Some of this extra testing is performed to determine the risk of altered DNA entering other organisms when products made from genetically modified organisms are discarded or released into the environment. Some tests evaluate if the unique chemistry of genetically modified foods cause allergies or produce metabolic effects. Tests on genetically modified organisms must also evaluate whether the modified DNA remains stable. Unstable DNA may undergo a genetic alteration called mutation, which can produce undesirable characteristics and make the organism potentially harmful. Certain religious agencies that determine the purity of foods and products do not recognize genetically modified products as being acceptable.

There is no reason to believe that GM foods pose public health safety problems. Most of the genes used in producing GM plants have no proven negative health effects on animals or people. Thus, the risk of getting cancer from GM foods is no greater than that for regular foods. GM foods, like any other foods, may pose food intolerance problems. Food intolerance occurs when a person cannot digest or break down a particular component of food. The food is either broken down into irritating compounds by intestinal bacteria, or it acts like a toxin in the blood. Some chemicals produced in GM animals and plants do cause intolerance in certain people. However, the same is true for natural dairy products that cause illness in people with an inherited condition called "lactose intolerance." GM organisms that pose this type of problem have limited use. For example, they may be restricted for use in animal feeds, industrial chemicals, or in other products that are not eaten by humans. People growing these organisms must provide evidence that the organisms are not being used to make food products.

Biotechnology Products and Environmental Safety

The chance of GM animals and plants causing environmental problems is a concern still under investigation. Scientists are currently studying two issues related to farming with GMOs. One issue deals with the problem of biodiversity decay due to GM invasion; the other concerns a phenomenon called **genetic pollution.**

Environmental groups around the world are criticizing the release of GMOs into farm fields and into nature because of the potential for invasiveness. Invasiveness refers to the ability of some organisms to take over or disrupt environments where they are normally not found. Dandelions and pigeons, which are common in almost every region of North America, are good examples of this. These organisms are native to Europe, but were accidently introduced to North America when the first European settlers reached America. These two organisms adapted very well to the conditions in North America. Some GMOs have a strong probability of being invasive and harming the local native organisms. **Biodiversity** is a measure of the number and variety of organisms in an environment. A decrease in biodiversity can permanently change the environment so that that the native organisms die off. This concern has led scientists to produce GMOs that have specific growing conditions that make it difficult or impossible for them to live in the wild.

Genetic pollution is a new concept for geneticists. The term refers to the transmission of engineered DNA from one organism to another. Genetic pollution is caused by **horizontal gene transmission** (**HGT**), which as we described in Chapter 3, is the transfer of genes from one organism to an unrelated organism. It can occur in various ways. In plants, HGT can occur through pollination, microbial transfer, or insect feeding transfer. Scientists have determined that pollen from genetically engineered corn in the United States and beets in Italy was transferred to other plants (Figure 8.2). Certain bacteria and fungi that attack the roots and leaves of plants can also transfer DNA from one plant to another. One of these bacteria, *Agrobacterium tumefaciens*, is used to transfer DNA from plant to plant in genetic engineering research. Some insects feed by biting into plants and sucking out the nutrient-rich sap that flows through the stems and leaves. These insects are known to pass diseases from one plant to another. Some scientists believe that DNA can be transferred between plants as the insects visit and feed upon different plants. So far there is no direct research evidence supporting this process of DNA transfer. Researchers have shown that DNA can be transferred between animals through eating. In one study, the intestinal cells of rats took up specially made gene sequences placed in their food.

HGT between animals is not proven to be a problem. It is theoretically possible that it could occur if a GM animal bred with a normal one, but no fertile GM animals have been released into the wild. Released GM animals, such as transgenic fish, are designed to

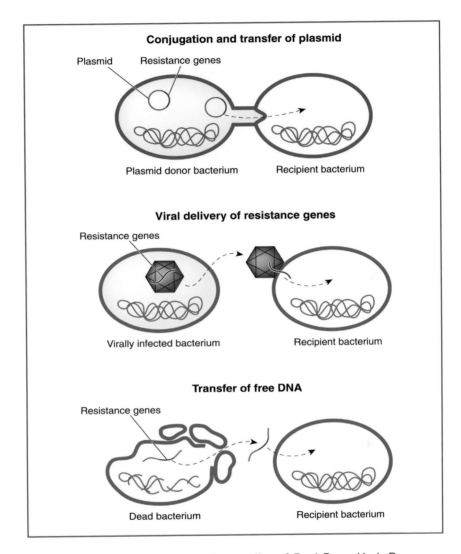

Figure 8.2 The genetic engineering studies of Paul Berg, Herb Boyer, Annie Chang, and Stanley Cohen raised the first biotechnology safety issues. They showed how DNA can be transferred from one organism to another both in nature and through laboratory techniques. Researchers then recognized that it was also possible for genetically modified organisms to pass along their DNA to other organisms. Three methods of DNA transfer are illustrated here.

be reproductively sterile so that they cannot pass along their transgenic DNA. This prevents any possibility of eggs, or sperm from GMOs spreading engineered DNA to other organisms.

ETHICAL AND MORAL ISSUES OF BIOTECHNOLOGY

The ethical issues of agricultural biotechnology have different considerations than the safety issues. Ethical issues deal with the "good" and "bad" decisions of a society. In many cases it is easy to balance the "good" and "bad" consequences of a technology. For example, vitamin A enriched rice can be considered a good agricultural development because it may reduce malnutrition. So, the rice may save the lives of many children in developing nations. This benefit, however, has some costs. First, vitamin A rice, called Golden Rice, might be expensive and farmers in poor countries may not be able to grow it without getting some type of government subsidy. These governments have limited financial resources, so they would have to restrict the rice to certain farms. Farmers who do not grow Golden Rice may be at a disadvantage and may lose their livelihood. Furthermore, much of the money made from biotechnology crop sales in developing nations funds the wealthy countries that have the economic ability to produce these new technologies.

A related issue in some developing countries is the use of GM crops to produce foods that are not part of the country's cultural eating habits. The GM crops are grown because they grow well and provide adequate food, but on many farms they are replacing natural crops of native foods that could be bred to grow well. Little effort is being put toward improving the native foods because scientists in those countries are not given financial support or incentive to do the research. Developing nations view this as a remnant of the days when their countries were colonized by imperial nations.

Another ethical issue deals with the increasing trend for scientists to use biotechnology to solve a variety of problems. Many scientists believe that this emphasis gives unfair advantages to those who do biotechnology research. The concern is that biotechnology research may overshadow equally feasible traditional approaches that may actually be safer, better, and less expensive to develop. Many scientists criticize the fact that research funding is focusing too much on biotechnology. For all the good that biotechnology brings, it may prove costly in the long term if traditional or alternative research becomes neglected.

Ethical considerations frequently influence how environmental and medical decisions are made, and thus significantly affect how biotechnology research progresses. The "good" and "bad" outcomes of agricultural and industrial biotechnology are weighed using measurements called "cost-benefit analyses." For example, the government of India may decide not to let an industrial biotechnology facility operate in a region. Their decision could be based on the balance of economic gain compared to the health and environmental problems that would result from an accident. Canadian agricultural officials might reject the use of a biotechnology vaccine for cattle because the economic loss caused by disease is outweighed by human health risks of the vaccine.

The scientific method practiced by researchers does not take into account the moral issues of different cultures. For example, some people of the Jewish and Muslim faiths are concerned whether GMOs can be eaten because they view it as unnatural according to their religious teachings. Consequently, biotechnology has limited applications in regions predominated by people of these faiths. People opposed to **abortion** may not want technologies that use cells taken from human embryos. Many advocates of natural foods oppose unusual or unnatural combinations of DNA in animals and plants. People holding these beliefs would prefer to ban transgenic technology, and would certainly avoid products made using this technology. Standards of morality vary from culture to culture. Thus, the acceptance of agricultural and industrial biotechnology will differ from culture to culture.

MISUSE OF BIOTECHNOLOGY

As with any innovation or invention, there is the potential for a legitimate idea or process to be put to inappropriate or illegal use. Biotechnology, like many other branches of science, is no exception. In 2004, the governments of Columbia and the United States discovered evidence of illegal consumer biotechnology operations. They found evidence that cocoa plants grown for the drug cocaine were being genetically modified to produce more of the drug. It is believed that scientists were hired to work in illegal laboratories specializing in making new drug plants.

Stop and Consider

Which of the following would be the greatest challenge for biotechnology?
- **Developing a GMO that fulfills the public's safety concerns.**
- **Developing a GMO that fulfills the public's ethical concerns.**
- **Developing a GMO that fulfills the public's moral concerns.**

CONNECTIONS

The advent of modern genetics was established in 1905 when William Bateson coined the term genetics. Genetic research opened the door for the early biotechnology endeavors taking place in the 1970s. Much of the scientific community greeted the new findings growing out of the biotechnology field. In turn, many scientists adopted biotechnology into their research, greatly enhancing the knowledge in many fields of biology and chemistry. Biotechnology innovations were working their way into society long before the public was aware of the term and the science behind its applications. At first, the public responded to biotechnology with distrust. This encouraged the government to seek out resolutions to the societal issues raised by biotechnology. The controversial issues raised by biotechnology can be classified into three categories: safety issues, ethical issues, and moral issues.

caused by StarLink. Studies undertaken to see if StarLink caused an **allergic response** were negative. Without intending to, the CDC demonstrated that StarLink was safe for human consumption; the manufacturers were hoping that the CDC studies provided sufficient evidence for StarLink to be approved for use in human foods. However, to this date no decision has been made about permiting the use of StarLink for human consumption. The StarLink debate is not over. In 2005, Syngenta told the federal government that 150 square kilometres of crops intended for human consumption were accidentally sown with wrong seeds. The seeds were from Bt11 corn which is not approved for human consumption.

What Are the Issues?

The StarLink incident raises several concerns about the regulations governing the safety of genetically modified (GM) foods. One concern is that the tight regulations enforced by the government did not prevent a potentially dangerous mistake. Luckily, in this instance, the mistake did not cause any health problems. This incident raises questions about whether existing guidelines are sufficient to protect public health. In response to the StarLink incident, some people have renewed the argument that all genetically modified organisms (GMOs) should be banned until a failsafe way is developed to keep incidents such as this from happening again. Other people further question the government's efforts at ensuring food security. The StarLink incident suggests that it might be possible for terrorists to contaminate a large segment of the food supply.

Stop and Consider

What are your views on the benefits of growing GM foods? How do you feel about eating transgenic plants that contain animal genes? What about eating transgenic plants that contain genes from a disease-causing bacterium?

People who support the use of GM food see the StarLink as a victory. Many supporters of GM foods believe that is a groundless fear of GMOs that drives most of the strict regulations on GM foods. These people note that many animals and crops are banned for food use with no scientific evidence backing the decisions. The StarLink incident may provide an incentive to base food safety regulations on sound research and not on probable safety concerns. So far, more and more GM foods eaten by animals and people throughout the world have not produced any noticeable increase in illnesses (Figure 9.2). However, the limited testing done by the CDC was not sufficient to clear StarLink corn for human consumption

CASE STUDY 2: TRANSGENIC CROPS AND THE DECLINE OF MONARCH BUTTERFLIES?

Background

Laboratory experiments on GMOs are conducted in special facilities designed to prevent the unintentional release of the organisms into the environment. Regulations dating to 1972 recommended strict guidelines on handling GM DNA and organisms. These regulations were voluntarily developed because nobody knew the outcomes of releasing novel DNA into the environment. Some biologists were concerned that GM DNA could be incorporated into naturally existing organisms. This effect might impart deleterious traits into these organisms. By the 1980s, the governments of many nations had set mandatory guidelines for producing and handling GMOs. The advent of agricultural biotechnology, however, made it necessary for certain GM organisms to be released into agricultural fields and pastures. After all, it would be very difficult and expensive to grow large fields of GM crops in greenhouses! Plus, it would be equally difficult to keep herds of GM domesticated animals in enclosed pens. So, the science of field-testing is applied to these GMOs to ensure their success under traditional growing conditions.

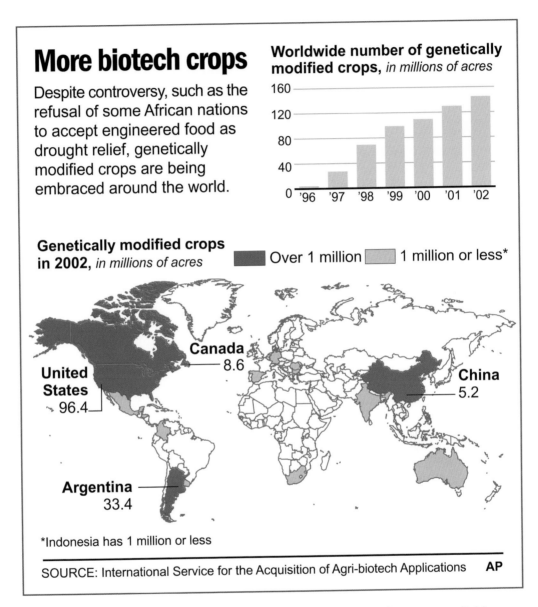

More biotech crops

Worldwide number of genetically modified crops, *in millions of acres*

Despite controversy, such as the refusal of some African nations to accept engineered food as drought relief, genetically modified crops are being embraced around the world.

Genetically modified crops in 2002, *in millions of acres*

Over 1 million ☐ 1 million or less*

Canada
8.6

United
States
96.4

China
5.2

Argentina
33.4

*Indonesia has 1 million or less

SOURCE: International Service for the Acquisition of Agri-biotech Applications   **AP**

Figure 9.2 Biotechnology crops are on the rise globally. Very few were available in 1987. Today there are over 150 GMO crops grown throughout the world. Many of the traits put into these crops protect them from drought, pests, and poor growing conditions.

The first field tests on GM crops met with much objection in almost every country conducting the trials. Food safety advocates and environmental groups staged protests that resulted in the various governments putting restrictions on the tests. Some protestors went as far as burning fields of research crops in India, Italy, and the United States. Many scientists also opposed the practice. They provided sound reasons why field-testing should not be done or should be very closely monitored. They stated that GMOs could get loose and cause environmental problems similar to those encountered when nonnative plants and animals become introduced into regions where they are not normally found. Second, they argued that DNA could become incorporated into related organisms by way of horizontal gene transfer discussed earlier in the book. Many biologists belief the the genetically engineered genes could negatively affect the survival of wildlife if the genes were incorporated into their cells. A third argument was that the organisms could have unintentional effects. This means that they can produce a variety of unforeseen problems if they accidently escape the fields into the nearby environment. One concern is that they can harm beneficial animals feeding on the GM crops. Another concern is that crops released into the wild may compete with related native plants disrupting the areas biodiversity.

One apparently unforeseen problem did arise in 1999 with a GM corn with a Bt gene, which was bred to produce a toxic protein to help it fight off one of its primary insect pests. Bt corn became the recipient of considerable negative media coverage when it was learned that its genetically engineered toxin may have been responsible for a decline in the populations of monarch butterflies (Figuer 9.3). Scientists determined that the butterflies, like the insect pests Bt corn was designed to destroy, could be killed by pollen from the GM plant. This concern came about when researchers monitoring the butterflies noticed an unexplainable decline in their population starting in the late

Figure 9.3 Scientists believed that the Bt toxin in Bt corn was causing a decline in the monarch butterfly population. It appeared that the monarch butterfly population was dropping at the same time Bt corn was being field tested and grown. Studies were conducted to see if pollen from Bt corn could kill a variety of butterflies and other beneficial insects. The studies exonerated Bt corn from being a cause of butterfly death.

1990s. Most monarch butterflies in North America migrate to the southernmost states and Mexico in the winter, where they feed and mate until they return north in the spring and summer to produce offspring. It was a large population in Mexico that showed the decline. The butterflies in Mexico are known to migrate through cornfields throughout the Midwest. Almost 30% of these fields had Bt corn.

Two researchers independently conducted experiments investigating the effects of Bt corn on monarch butterflies. In these studies, milkweed plants—the preferred food of monarch butterflies—were dusted with pollen from Bt corn It was shown that toxin-containing pollen from Bt corn settled on milkweed growing near fields where the GM corn grown. It was theorized that the butterflies picked up the toxin from contaminated milkweed. Initial studies showed that large concentrations of this toxin could kill monarch butterfly caterpillars feeding on plants dusted pollen from several varieties of Bt corn. In one study conducted at Cornell University, researchers discovered that 44% of the monarch butterflies that fed on contaminated milkweed died. Similar studies conducted at several universities yielded similar findings for other insects not targeted by Bt. Particularly compelling were studies carried out by Karen Oberhauser at the University of Minnesota.

PRO or CON?

GMO Corn

The intensive government study done on the people who ate StarLink corn showed that it was very likely safe for human consumption. After all, research also showed that it did not harm any of the animals that fed on the corn. What are the pros and cons of using the CDC's StarLink corn study to allow more GMO crops to be used for human consumption? What are your feelings about the debate?

Oberhauser discovered that Bt corn pollen could spread into the environment carrying the Bt toxin inside of it. This in turn could harm insects feeding on plants dusted with the pollen. She published this data in a prestigious journal called the *Proceedings of the National Academy of Sciences.* Studies conducted by researchers at the USDA did not support these results, however. They concluded that Bt corn was unlikely to have caused the high decline in monarchs and other insects. The USDA believed that the amount of pollen that could have been eaten by the monarchs would not been enough to kill these insects. Their experiments modeled the type of exposure to Bt corn pollen monarch butterflies were likely to encounter in nature. The Cornell group and other studies apparently used exceedingly large amounts of pollen in a laboratory setting. Considering the conflicting data, the scientific community ultimately agreed that there was not enough evidence to support claims that Bt corn was responsible for the monarch population problems.

Stop and Consider

How would you propose balancing the benefits and risks of raising GMOs outside of a laboratory?

What Are the Issues?

Scientific investigations of environmental factors are not simple studies to conduct. In many cases, the data do not always produce conclusive, irrefutable evidence. That is why it is very difficult to blame illnesses suffered by animals and humans on pollution. The studies on the effects of Bt corn were not exempt from this limitation. In one group of studies, Bt corn contamination was found to kill insects that are important to the environment. Many of these insects feed on pest insects. Others are **pollinators**, meaning that they may be the only mechanism by which certain plants can reproduce. Clover and other plants used for animal feed and honey production are suffering because of declining bee populations. The bees that pollinate clover are dying as a result of exposure to agricultural pesticides. Many honey producers have to regularly import bees to replace those killed by the pesticides from nearby farms.

Stop and Consider

What experiments would you want to see performed to evaluate whether plants containing a GM toxin create fewer environmental problems than pesticides?

People who oppose the release of Bt corn believe that its pollen has the potential to create environmental problems. Supporters of Bt corn, on the other hand, believe that the corn should not be banned based on data that they consider to be preliminary. They feel that comprehensive studies are needed to show that the GM corn is harmful. After all, Bt corn technology reduces the need for pesticides—and there is conclusive and inarguable evidence that

PRO or CON?

StarLink Corn and Monarch Butterflies

The scare about Bt corn harming monarch butterflies proved to be based on inconclusive science. Further investigations quelled the issue, showing that proper science should be done before assuming the negative impacts of any technology. A similar issue arises when GMO bacteria and plants are used for environmental clean-up. Some studies show that these organisms can do as much harm as good. What are the pros and cons of using inconclusive scientific data to address concerns about biotechnology applications?

agricultural pesticides adversely affect many types of beneficial insects, including monarch butterflies. The decline of bee populations in the United States is irrefutably due to pesticides. Farmers who use fewer pesticides have seen a recovery of local bee populations.

CONNECTIONS

Case studies are powerful tools used to train people how to resolve complex issues. Attorneys and medical doctors are presented with many case studies before they graduate and go into practice. Their case studies provide a safe environment to practice important decisions that are best not learned on the job. Many government officials and policy makers use case studies to help them make decisions about new laws or regulations. Case studies work best when they are realistic and do not lead to simple resolutions of the issues being analyzed. Many biotechnology companies use case studies for their specific industries to help them better understand the issues related to new developments. This has particular importance in the safety, ethical, and moral concerns of biotechnology. Case studies help biotechnology developers become better aware of the ramifications of their products. Plus, they can be used to educate the public and policy makers about the benefits and risks of biotechnology.

FOR MORE INFORMATION

For more information about the concepts discussed in this chapter, search the Web using the following keywords:

Kraft Foods, StarLink corn, Monarch Butterfly, Environmental effects of biotechnology, Health effects of biotechnology, Bt corn

c. 4000-2000 B.C. Yeast used to leaven bread and make beer and wine

c. 500 B.C. Moldy soybean curds used to treat boils (first antibiotic)

c. 8000 B.C. Crops and livestock domesticated

c. 100 A.D. Powdered chrysanthemums used as first insecticide

1590 Microscope invented

1600 Beginning of the Industrial Revolution in Europe

1663 Cells discovered

1675 Anton van Leeuwenhoek discovers bacteria

1797 Edward Jenner inoculates child to protect him from smallpox

1857 Louis Pasteur proposes microbe theory for fermentation

1859 Charles Darwin published the theory of evolution through natural selection

1865 Gregor Mendel published the results of his studies on heredity in peas

1890 Walther Fleming discovers chromosomes

1914 First use of bacteria to treat sewage

1919 Term biotechnology was coined by Karl Ereky, a Hungarian engineer

1922 First person injected with insulin, obtained from a cow

1928 Alexander Fleming discovers penicillin

1933 Hybrid corn commercialized

1944 Oswald Avery, Colin MacLeod, and Maclyn McCarty prove that DNA carries genetic information

1953 James Watson and Francis Crick publish paper describing the structure of DNA

1961 *Bacillus thuringiensis* registered as first biopesticide

1966 Marshall Warren Nirenberg, Har Gobind Korhana, and Robert Holley, figure out the genetic code

1973 Herbert Boyer and Stanley Cohen construct first recombinant DNA molecule and reproduce

1975 First monoclonal antibodies produced

1975 Asilomar Conference held; participants urge U.S. government to develop guidelines for work with recombinant DNA

1977 Human gene expressed in bacteria

1977 Method developed for rapid sequencing of long stretches of DNA

1978 Recombinant human insulin produced

1980 U.S. Supreme Court allows the Chakrabarty patent for a bacterium able to break down oil because it contains two different plasmids

1980 Stanley Cohen and Herbert Boyer awarded first patent for cloning a gene; Paul Berg, Walter Gilbert, and Frederick Sanger awarded Nobel Prize in chemistry for the creation of the first recombinant molecule

1981 First transgenic animals (mice) produced

1982 Human insulin, first recombinant biotech drug, approved by the FDA

1983 Human immunodeficiency virus, the cause of AIDS, is identified by U.S. and French scientists

1983 Idea for PCR conceived by Kary Mullis, an American molecular biologist

1984 First DNA based method for genetic fingerprinting developed by Alec Jeffreys

1985 First field testing of transgenic plants resistant to insects, bacteria and viruses

1985 Recombinant human growth hormone approved by the FDA

1985 Scientists discovered that some patients who had received human growth disorder hormone from cadavers had died of a rare brain disorder

1986 First recombinant cancer drug approved, interferon

1987 The first field test of a recombinant bacterium, Frostban, engineered to inhibit ice formation

1988 Human Genome Project funded by Congress

1990 Recombinant enzyme for making cheese introduced, becoming the first recombinant product in the U.S. food supply

1990 First human gene therapy performed, in an effort to treat a child with an immune disorder

1990 Insect resistant Bt corn approved

1994 First gene for susceptibility to breast cancer discovered

1994 First recombinant food (FlavrSavr tomatoes) approved by FDA

1994 Recombinant bovine growth hormone (bovine somatotropin, BST)

1997 Weed killer resistant soybeans and insect resistant cotton commercialized

1997 Dolly the sheep, the first animal cloned from an adult cell, is born

1998 Rough draft of human gene map produced, placing 30,000 genes

1999 Jesse Gelsinger, a participant in a gene therapy trial for an inherited enzyme defect, dies as a result of the treatment

2000 First report of gene therapy "cures" for an inherited immune system defect. A few months later, several of the treated children developed a blood cancer

2002 Draft of human genome sequence completed

2003 First endangered species cloned (the banteng, a wild ox of Southeast Asia)

2003 Dolly, the cloned sheep, develops a serious chronic lung disease and is euthanized

2003 Japanese scientists develop a genetically engineered coffee plant the produces low caffeine beans

2004 Korean scientists report human embryonic stem cell produced using a nucleus from an adult cell

2005 Korean scientists improve success rate of human adult nuclear transfer to embryonic cells by 10 fold

Abortion—The destruction of a fetus before it finishes developing.

Adenosine deaminase deficiency—A defect in certain immune system cells that prevents the body from fighting disease.

Agriculture—The activities and technologies involved in growing plants and animals for commerce and food. Farming is the most common form of agriculture.

Allergy—An oversensitive immune response to a foreign substance in or on the body.

Allergic response—The characteristic signs of an allergy. It may include itching, rash, sneezing, or watery eyes.

Amino acid—Biochemical that is the building block of proteins.

Anemia—A disease characterized by abnormal or a decreased number of red blood cells.

Antibodies—Proteins produced by the immune system used to fight disease.

Antigen—A substance that triggers the immune system to generate an immune response.

Antioxidant—Any of a group of chemicals that slow the natural decay of substances by stopping the degradative effects of oxygen.

Artificial insemination—A breeding technique in which sperm from a male animal is collected and introduced into a female animal under controlled conditions.

Bacteria—A class of single-celled microscopic organisms; many forms feed on dead matter or live as a pathogen on or in plants or animals.

Biochemical—Any of several complex molecules found mostly in organisms; biochemicals belong to a group of chemicals called organic molecules.

Biodegradable—Having the ability to break down rapidly or easily into harmless chemicals.

Biodiversity—A measure of the number of types of organisms in an environment.

Bioinformatics—The use of computers to manage biological information.

Bionanotechnology—The science of developing miniature computers and machines from biochemicals and components of organisms.

Bioprocessing—The use of cells, components of cells, or microorganisms to create commercially important products or perform commercially important processes.

Bioreactor—A container for synthesizing biochemicals.

Bioremediation—A technique using cells, cell components, or microorganisms such as bacteria and yeast to break down wastes. Also called environmental bioprocessing.

Bioremediation agent—A biochemical or microorganism capable of safely breaking down a waste product.

Biotechnology—Any technique that uses living organisms (or their components) to make or modify products, improve plants and animals, or develop microorganisms for specific, practical use.

Breeder—A person who breeds animals or plants for particular uses.

Breeding—The process of mating.

Bt toxin—An insecticidal protein produced in the bacteria, *Bacillus thuringiensis*.

Carbohydrate—Any of the various biochemicals consisting of carbon, oxygen, and hydrogen that include the sugars and starches and are a major source of energy in organisms.

Centrifuge—A machine that separates chemicals in a mixture by spinning them at high speeds.

Chiral isomers—Mirror image. Some molecules exist having alternate shapes called chiral forms. The molecules are, in effect, mirror images of each other.

Chimera—An organism that contains cells from two different organisms or species.

Chromatography—A technique for separating the components of a mixture based on the difference in how the components travel through a filter-like material.

Chromosome—A strand of DNA that carries genes and is responsible for passing hereditary information from the parents to the offspring.

Compound nucleic acid—A chain of nucleic acids.

Deoxyribonucleic acid (DNA)—Nucleic acid that contains an organism's genetic information.

Direct products—Industrial products that are used directly by consumers.

DNA—See deoxyribonucleic acid.

Domestication—The process of altering a plant or animal through selection to make it more valuable for human use.

Dominant—A gene that almost always produces the physical characteristic it codes for, even when combined with a gene that codes for a different characteristic.

Embryo—An organism during the early stages of development that immediately follows fertilization.

Embryo splitting—A process in which the cells of an embryo are separated and grown to produce multiple embryos. It was the earliest form of cloning developed in the 1970s.

Enzyme—A protein that performs or increases the speed of specific chemical reactions.

Enzyme linked immunosorbant assay—Also known as ELISA, this technique uses enzymes to identify specific chemicals.

Erythropoietin—A hormone in the body that stimulates the production of red blood cells.

Expression—The means by which information in a gene is converted into the chemistry and structure present in a cell.

Extraction—A method for separating chemicals from a mixture.

Fat—A group of biochemicals composed mostly of carbon and hydrogen atoms. Most fats do not dissolve in water.

Fermentation—A chemical process in which microorganisms split an organic chemical into simpler substances.

Filter—A material used to separate solids from a liquid.

Fungi—A diverse group of organisms usually composed of cells formed into branched filaments. Fungi feed primarily on decaying matter. The singular is fungus.

Gene—A segment of DNA that contains the genetic information for a particular trait.

Genetic engineering—Biotechnology techniques used to modify an organism's genetic material or combine genetic material from one or more organisms to change an organism's characteristics.

Genetically modified organism (GMO)—Any organism whose characteristics were changed using genetic engineering.

Genetic material—The hereditary material of an organism that programs for its traits.

Genetic pollution—The transmission of engineered DNA from one organism to another.

Genome—An organism's complete genetic information.

GMO—See genetically modified organism.

HGT—See horizontal gene transmission.

Horizontal gene transmission (HGT)—The natural passage of DNA from one organism to an unrelated organism. It is most commonly transferred through pollination and ingestion.

Hormone—Any of a group of biochemicals (usually proteins) produced in the body that control certain functions in the body.

Hybrid—An offspring of two organisms of different races, breeds, varieties, species, or genera.

Hybridization—The breeding of genetically dissimilar organisms to produce offspring with new characteristics.

Indirect products—Industrial materials that are used in the manufacturing of consumer products.

***In situ* environmental bioprocessing**—Environmental cleanup that is performed using microorganisms or biochemicals at the site of the pollution.

***In vitro* fertilization**—A breeding technique in which selected sperm and eggs are united under laboratory conditions rather than inside the body.

Irrigation—To supply land with water, usually for agricultural uses.

Keratin—A protein used to strengthen hair and nails. It is also found in skin.

Mad cow disease—An infectious brain disease of cattle.

Malnutrition—A condition caused by insufficient nutrients in the diet. It usually causes a person to succumb to other diseases.

Metabolism—The chemical reactions that carry out the living functions of an organism.

Metallurgy—The science of obtaining and preparing metal for practical use.

Microarray—A collection of DNA or protein samples that can be bound to other chemicals to study patterns of gene expression.

Microorganism—An organism that must be viewed through a microscope to be seen. Bacteria and fungi are examples of microorganisms.

Molecule—A chemical made up of two or more atoms.

Monoculture—The agricultural practice of growing large amounts of one variety of an animal or plant.

Nanomachines—Microscopic machines composed of biological molecules.

Nanotechnology—The science of developing miniature computers and machines.

Nucleic acid—An organic chemical belonging to a complex group of molecules that form the genetic material and fuel metabolism.

Nucleotide—The building block of nucleic acids. They are made up of either a ribose or deoxyribose sugar that attaches to a phosphate group.

Organism—Any life form.

Pharming—The use of genetically modified organisms for the production of medications.

Phytoremediation—The use of plants for bioremediation.

Plasmid—A fragment of DNA that exists independently of an organism's genomic DNA. They are mostly found in bacteria and are used in recombinant DNA research.

Platform—A method of carrying out an industrial activity.

Pollinator—An organism or event that transfers pollen from one plant to another. Insects and wind are common pollinators.

Protein—A complex biochemical composed of chains of amino acids. Proteins provide function and structure for organisms.

Recessive—A gene that produces the physical characteristic it codes for only in the absence of other genes that code for different characteristics.

Recombinant DNA—Genetically engineered DNA.

Recombinant DNA technology—Techniques that combine the DNA of two different organisms.

Ribonucleic acid (RNA)—A single-stranded nucleic acid made up of a chain of nucleotides and containing a ribose sugar component. It is involved in gene expression.

RNA—See ribonucleic acid.

Selective breeding—Mating animals and plants with similar characteristics to produce large uniform populations that consistently breed those features.

Stem cell—An animal cell capable of developing into other types of cells.

Stem borer—One of many insects the eat their way into the stems of crops.

Sterilization—The destruction of all microorganisms on a surface or in an area. Also the term used for the process of rendering an organism incapable of reproduction.

Storage proteins—Proteins in the body used as a reserve when the diet falls low in proteins or amino acids.

Superbug—A bioremediation term referred to bacteria capable of rapidly degrading pollutants.

Supercomputer—A series of computers designed to work as one rapidly operating computer with a large amount of memory.

Surrogate—A female animal used to carry offspring introduced by *in vitro* fertilization.

Tissue—A body structure composed of groups of cells. Tissues carry out specific functions in the body.

Trait—A specific characteristic of an organism.

Transfected—Cells that are genetically altered.

Transfection vector—A piece of DNA used to introduce genes into animals and plants.

Transgenic—A genetically modified organism that has DNA inserted from an unrelated organism.

Transistor—A small device that controls the flow of electricity through an electric circuit.

Vector—An artificial chromosome used in recombinant DNA technology to introduce DNA into the cells of animals, fungi, and plants.

Yeast—A specific kind of fungi.

Yield—The amount of usable food produced by an agricultural animal or plant.

Burden, David W., and Donald B. Whitney. *Biotechnology: Proteins to PCR: A Course in Strategies and Lab Techniques.* Cambridge, MA: Birkhauser Boston, 1995.

Chrispeels, Maarten J., and David E. Sadava. *Plants, Genes, and Crop Biotechnology* (2nd Edition). Sudbury, MA: Jones and Bartlett Publishers, 2002.

Cipolla, Carlo M. *Before the Industrial Revolution: European Society and the Economy.* New York, NY: W.W. Norton & Company, 1994.

Committee on Science, Subcommittee on Technology, U.S. House of Representatives. *Industrial Biotechnology: A Solution for the Future?* Washington, DC: U.S. Government Printing Office, 1998.

Deane, Phyllis. *The First Industrial Revolution* (2nd Edition). Cambridge, England, UK: Cambridge University Press, 1980.

Demain, Arnold L., and Julian Davies, editors. *Manual of Industrial Microbiology and Biotechnology.* Washington, DC: American Society of Microbiology, 1999.

Diamond, Jared. *Guns, Germs, and Steel: The Fates of Human Societies.* New York, NY: W.W. Norton & Company, 1999.

Freifelder, David. *Applications to Biochemistry and Molecular Biology.* New York, NY.: W.H. Freeman and Company, 1976.

Glazer, Alexander N., and Hiroshi Nikaido. *Microbial Biotechnology.* New York, NY: W.H. Freeman & Company, 1995.

Glick, Bernard R., and Jack J. Pasternak. *Molecular Biotechnology: Principles and Applications of Recombinant DNA.* Washington, DC: American Society of Microbiology, 2003.

Goodsell, David S. *Bionanotechnology: Lessons from Nature.* New York, NY: Wiley-Liss, 2004.

Gupta, Manju, and Raghav Ram. "Development of Genetically Modified Crops," In *GMO Handbook, Genetically Modified Animals, Microbes, and Plants in Biotechnology.* Sarad R. Parekh, ed. Totowa, NY: Humana Press, 2004.

Harlan, Jack Rodney. *The Living Fields: Our Agricultural Heritage.* Cambridge, England, UK: Cambridge University Press, 1998.

Kreuzer, Helen, and Adrianne Massey. *Recombinant DNA and Biotechnology.* Washington, DC: American Society of Microbiology, 1996.

Lydersen, Bjorn K., Nancy A. D'Elia, and Kim L. Nelson, eds. *Bioprocess Engineering.* New York, NY: Wiley-Interscience, 1994.

Rittmann, Bruce E., and Perry L. McCarty. *Environmental Biotechnology: Principles and Applications.* New York, NY: McGraw-Hill Science/ Engineering/Math, 2000.

Slater, Adrian, Nigel W. Scott, and Mark R. Fowler. *Plant Biotechnology: The Genetic Manipulation of Plants.* Oxford, England, UK: Oxford University Press, 2003.

Stearns, Peter N. *The Industrial Revolution in World History.* Boulder, CO: Perseus Books, 1993.

Uhlig, Helmut, ed. *Industrial Enzymes and Their Applications.* New York, NY: Wiley Interscience, 1998.

Winston, Mark L. *Travels in the Genetically Modified Zone.* Cambridge, MA: Harvard University Press, 2002.

Whitford, William. "Large-Scale Exogenous Protein Production in Higher Animal Cells," In *GMO Handbook, Genetically Modified Animals, Microbes, and Plants in Biotechnology.* Sarad R. Parekh, ed. Totowa, NY: Humana Press, 2004.

RESOURCES

The following readings provide detailed backgrounds of agriculture, biotechnology, and industrial manufacturing. Some of these resources investigate the ethical and legal issues of biotechnology.

BOOKS

Borem, Aluzio, Fabricio R. Santos, and David E. Bowen. *Understanding Biotechnology.* San Francisco, CA: Prentice Hall, 2003.

Bourgaize, David, Thomas R. Jewell, and Rodolfo G. Buiser. *Biotechnology: Demystifying the Concepts.* San Francisco, CA: Pearson Education, 1999.

Chrispeels, Maarten J., and David E. Sadava. *Plants, Genes, and Crop Biotechnology* (2nd Edition). Sudbury, MA: Jones and Bartlett Publishers, 2002.

Fumento, Michael. *BioEvolution. How Biotechnology is Changing the World.* San Francisco, CA: Encounter Books, 2003.

Glazer, Alexander N., and Hiroshi Nikaido. *Microbial Biotechnology.* New York, NY: W.H. Freeman & Company, 1995.

Herren, Ray V. *The Science of Agriculture: A Biological Approach.* Stamford, CT: Delmar Learning, 2000.

Rabinow, Paul. *Making PCR: A Story of Biotechnology.* Chicago, IL: University of Chicago Press, 1997.

Scheppler, Judith A., Patricia E. Cassin, and Rosa M. Gambler. *Biotechnology Explorations: Applying the Fundamentals.* Washington, DC: American Society of Microbiology, 2000.

Thieman, William J., Michael A. Palladino, and William Thieman. *Introduction to Biotechnology.* San Francisco, CA: Benjamin Cummings, 2003.

The following readings provide detailed backgrounds of agriculture, biotechnology, and industrial manufacturing. Some of these resources investigate the ethical and legal issues of biotechnology.

Borem, A., F.R. Santos, & D.E. Bowen. 2003. *Understanding Biotechnology.* Prentice Hall; San Francisco, CA.

Bourgaize, D., T.R. Jewell, & R.G. Buiser. 1999. *Biotechnology: Demystifying the Concepts.* Pearson Education: San Francisco, CA.

Chrispeels, M.J. and D.E. Sadava. 2002. *Plants, Genes, and Crop Biotechnology.* 2nd Edition. Jones and Bartlett Publishers: Sudbury, MA.

Furmento, M. 2003. BioEvolution. How *Biotechnology is Changing the World.* Encounter Books: San Francisco, CA.

Glazer, A.N. & N. Hiroshi. 1995. *Microbial Biotechnology.* W.H. Freeman: New York, NY.

Herren, R.V. 2000. *The Science of Agriculture: A Biological Approach.* Delmar Learning: Stamford, CT.

Rabinow, P. 1997. *Making PCR: A Story of Biotechnology.* University of Chicago Press: Chicago, IL.

Scheppler, J.A., P.E. Cassin, & R.M. Gambler. 2000. *Biotechnology Explorations: Applying the Fundamentals.* American Society of Microbiology: Washington, DC.

Thieman, W.J., M.A. Palladamo, and W. Thieman. 2003. *Introduction to Biotechnology.* Benjamin Cummings: San Francisco, CA.

Access Excellence
http://www.accessexcellence.org

ActionBioscience
http://www.actionbioscience.org

BioCom
http://www.biocom.org

BioTech: Life Sciences Resources and Reference Tools
http://biotech.icmb.utexas.edu

Biotechnology Institute
http://www.biotechinstitute.org

Cold Spring Harbor Laboratory
http://www.cshl.org

Council for Biotechnology Information
http://www.whybiotech.com

Food and Nutrition Information Center
http://www.nal.usda.gov/fnic/

Information Systems for Biotechnology
http://www.isb.vt.edu

National Center for Biotechnology Information
http://www.ncbi.nlm.nih.gov

Pew Initiative on Food and Biotechnology
http://pewagbiotech.org

Transgenic Crops: An Introduction and Resource Guide
http://www.colostate.edu/programs/lifesciences/TransgenicCrops/

page:

BRIAN SHMAEFSKY is a professor of biology and environmental sciences at Kingwood College near Houston, Texas. He did his undergraduate studies in biology at Brooklyn College in New York and completed masters and doctoral studies at Southern Illinois University at Edwardsville. His research emphasis is in environmental physiology. Dr. Shmaefsky has many publications on science education, some appearing in the *American Biology Teacher* and the *Journal of College Science Teaching*. He regularly consults on general biology and microbiology textbook projects. Dr. Shmaefsky is also very active serving on environmental awareness and policy committees in Mexico and Texas. He has two children, Kathleen, 14, and Timothy, 16, and lives in Kingwood with his dog Dusty.